TROUBLE
at OUR
DOOR

K I R K   S T E W A R T

PAGE PUBLISHING, INC.
New York, NY

First originally published by Page Publishing, Inc. 2016

ISBN 978-1-68289-798-0 (pbk)
ISBN 978-1-68289-799-7 (digital)

Printed in the United States of America

CHAPTER 1

FIRE

Bam bam bam bam bam bam! "Hello, is anybody home?" the voice said. I was just trying to come out of a deep sleep. I had only been in bed about four and a half hours. I had driven over eight hundred miles and collapsed in bed. Still groggy, I was slowly waking up.

Bam bam bam! Was someone bangin' on my front door? Were they at my door? I heard a voice say again, "Is anybody home?"

Did that voice come from outside my front door or from inside my house? It was loud. I heard the noise again. *Bam bam bam!* "Is anybody home?" the voice said. Yes, it was a real voice. It was a voice at my house. I wasn't dreaming.

I climbed out of bed and stepped into some sandals on the floor and headed for the front of the house. I shouted, "I'm coming. Just a minute."

As I turned into the small living room / den, I stepped over and opened the front door. Standing on my front porch was a young man in his early twenties wearing a blue bicycle riding suit—that is a tight latex short-sleeved shirt and matching latex blue riding shorts with a blue bicycle helmet. I could see his red hair peeking out from under his helmet. I remember how bright the sun was that day. After all, it was July 13, 1997. I could barely see at all at first because the sun was so bright. "Mister, your barn is on fire," he said. He pointed toward the old barn that stood about sixty feet west of the little prefabricated house we lived in. I had no idea how my life was about to change.

I stepped out onto the front porch and looked. Flames were shooting out of the roof of the old two-story barn. It seemed the flames were coming out of a section of the roof I knew to be open because a full-grown tree had fallen and a large branch had created a hole in the roof about the size of a small room.

I stepped back in the house, grabbed our portable phone, hit 911, and handed it to the young man who had awakened me. "Tell them there's a fire," I told him. I heard him saying, "What's the address? What's the address?" I shouted out the address but told him not to worry, that 911 would show the address when they received the call. I told him, "Just tell them there's a fire. They will have the address."

I went down the six steps that lead from the front porch and front door down to the ground. I moved over and turned on an outdoor faucet. A water hose was already attached to the faucet. I dragged the hose toward the old barn and began spraying. Immediately, I knew that wasn't going to help much, so I laid that hose down and ran around behind the house and grabbed a second hose attached to a faucet on the back of the house. I dragged it toward the barn, picked up the first hose, and began spraying water from both hoses up on the roof, where I saw the flames coming out and scorching the trees that were hanging over the old barn.

The front of the old barn was open, and as I looked into the old barn, my eyes fell on a large box. I knew that box contained the boys' and girls' track team uniforms from the school where I worked. I had just purchased them that spring through the school. I had brought them home to wash them so I could properly pack them away in storage at the school. I laid both hoses down and went into the old barn and retrieved the box with the track uniforms inside. They had not been damaged at all. I dragged the box away from the barn into the front yard under a tree. The only other thing I retrieved from the barn was a small box of photographs I had placed in an old bathtub to keep them safe when the floor of the old barn flooded when it rained.

Just as I picked up the hoses and started spraying again, a small explosion blew out the window upstairs on the front (north side) of the barn. It had been covered over on the inside by a sheet of black Sheetrock. I backed up a little bit but kept spraying water on the roof of the barn. I heard the sirens as the fire trucks drew nearer. It hadn't taken the fire department more than six or seven minutes to respond. As they began to arrive at the scene, I turned and saw ten to fifteen people standing around my front yard. Several cars had pulled over on the side of the busy six-lane highway that passed in front of my house. A hot mid-July Sunday morning had just gotten hotter.

CHAPTER 2

HOME EARLY

The reason I was even home on that Sunday morning was because a planned trip had fallen apart. My wife, Kara, and I had cut short a summer's last trip.

I was (and am) a schoolteacher, and the summer was quickly coming to an end. I had one more week before in-service training and another school year beginning. We had had a busy three or four weeks. I (Jack Phillips) and my wife (Kara Phillips) had been trying to make it to Kentucky Lake with some friends from Oak Grove, Kentucky, before the summer ended. Tim was in the military and trained helicopter pilots at Fort Campbell, Kentucky. He and his wife, Sheri, had become close friends of ours.

We had been at their home the two weekends before. On June 30, 1997, we were planning to go to the lake when we got a phone call and were told our daughter, Mary Lynn, was in labor and about to give birth to our fourth grandchild. We left Kentucky and drove back to Rector, Arkansas, our childhood home and the place where Mary Lynn and her family lived. That trip had proved unnecessary, and the labor a false alarm. We had actually planned to spend the night on Sunday, June 30, and go the lake with our friends on Monday and Tuesday (July 1 and 2) because Tim was off.

We were back home in Rector for the July 4 weekend holiday. We left on July 5 and went back to Nashville to spend the night. We headed up to Tim and Sheri's on the sixth with the intention of spending the night and going to the lake on the seventh and eighth. At about six o'clock that Sunday night, we received a call from Ricky Short, a friend staying at our home. He said someone had called and Mary Lynn was headed back to the hospital with labor pains. For the second weekend in a row, we made the long five-hour drive. We had to go to Poplar Bluff, Missouri, this time to the hospital where she had been admitted.

Mary Lynn gave birth to Michelle, our fourth grandchild, on the night of July 6. We made it to the hospital just before the birth. It had been a mad rush from Kentucky to the hospital in Missouri. Kara stayed on to help with the other grandchildren, Mary Lynn, and the newborn baby.

I returned to Memphis on Tuesday, July 8, planning on doing some honey-dos and trying to get the car checked out. I kept losing the charge on the battery. Tuesday night, at about 11:00 p.m., I received a call from Donna Tisdale. She and her husband, Timmy, were at the casino in Tunica, Mississippi. She said they had been there since Sunday. She was calling to ask me if they could stop by the house. She said Timmy had had a motorcycle wreck the week before and stuck a piece of wood completely through his thigh. She said it was bleeding and killing him and they needed a place to clean the wound and redress it before they drove back to Campbell, Missouri. I told them to come on and that I would wait up. I then received another call from some friends in Birmingham, Alabama. They were having a big pool party on Saturday afternoon to celebrate their twenty-fifth wedding anniversary. They wanted us to come. I told them we were already committed to going back to Kentucky on Sunday, July 13, but I would check with Kara and let them know if we could make it on Saturday or not. Timmy and Donna showed up and cleaned up the leg wound. It was a nasty hole about the size of quarter. The piece of wood had entered the inside of the thigh and exited the outside of the thigh. He was in quite a lot of pain. They left the house at about 1:30 a.m. Before they left, I did get Timmy to look at my car. He had me reconnect the ground wire on the alternator. He said that was probably causing all my electrical problems.

I went to bed at about one forty-five that morning and slept late on Wednesday morning.

I called Kara at Mary Lynn's about eight o'clock on Wednesday night. Everything was fine with Mary Lynn and the baby. They were home from the hospital and settled in. Kara had arranged some help for Mary Lynn. We discussed trying to go to Birmingham for the Saturday pool party and then going on to Oak Grove, Kentucky, for a few days at the lake. We would stay there on Monday and Tuesday and return to Memphis on Tuesday, July 15.

I hung up the phone and called Tim and Sheri and told them our plans. They said to come on and that the boat would be waiting. They congratulated me on the new grandbaby. I tried calling our friends in Birmingham, but I got no answer. I left a message on their answering machine that we were coming. They had said it might be hard to reach them but to come on anyway. I told them we would be staying at the Days' Inn in Fultondale, Alabama. Their children had all kinds of activities planned that weekend for their anniversary besides the pool party.

I left Memphis early Thursday morning and drove to Rector. I spent much of the day at Mary Lynn's, holding the new grandbaby and messing with the other grandchildren. What a delight! There was another granddaughter and two grandsons, so there was plenty to do. Paw Paw and Nanu had a wonderful time. We headed back to Memphis at about 8:00 p.m. on Thursday night.

We never could reach our friends in Birmingham by phone, but we left Friday to make the seven-hour drive there. The car was still acting up some, or we could have made the drive in five hours or so. We finally made it and checked into the Days' Inn at Fultondale, Alabama, a suburb of Birmingham. We were assigned room 206. We continued to call and try to reach our friends but never made contact, although we did leave them another message and tell them where we were.

Saturday morning, we drove to our friends' home, but no one was there. We called and called but got no answer. We kept expecting them to call us at the motel. I realized they had never actually said the party was at their house, although I knew they had a nice pool. We called Tim and Sheri to check in, and she said Tim had just taken a week's vacation so we could have some real fun. She said they were going to the lake Friday morning but would come home Saturday night to be with us and take us back to the lake with them on Sunday morning.

We never saw our friends in Birmingham, and we checked out of the motel at 11:55 a.m. on Saturday morning. We stopped and ate lunch just outside of Birmingham then headed north. It was a long drive, and we didn't roll into Tim and Sheri's driveway until about 6:00 p.m. on Saturday night. It was hot, hot, hot, and no one was home. We wrote a note and drove back down the interstate toward Nashville to an exit we had noticed coming in, where a big mall was located. We thought we would go hang out there in the air conditioning for a few hours and then check back.

The mall closed at 9:00 p.m., and we drove back to Tim and Sheri's. Surely they would be home by now. We pulled in the driveway and saw our note was still on the door. We decided to try to wait it out. At ten thirty, they still weren't home, and we faced a dilemma: we were broke. My pay would be automatically deposited on Monday, and we could withdraw all we wanted then. However, we didn't have enough cash for a motel room, and all we had were gas credit cards. We still had three days to spend on the lake. We sure didn't want to miss out a third time. We had a lot invested in this last vacation trip to the lake with our friends.

Truthfully, however, we were hot, tired, and pretty disgusted. Nothing we had planned had worked out. We had already missed our friends in Birmingham, and it looked like we had missed our friends in Kentucky too. Now we were stranded in the middle of the night outside our friends' home and burning up and being carried away by the mosquitoes. This wasn't how the last weekend of the summer was supposed to go.

We did still have our gas credit cards. We decided to just go back home and try to come back maybe on the Labor Day weekend. We wrote a new note and left it on the door, telling them we were going home.

We left there about 10:30 p.m. We used our gas credit cards to pay for gas, food, and drinks on the way back to Memphis. We got home about 3:00 a.m. on Sunday, July 13. I pulled the car around back to unload the suitcases and to avoid the six steps on the front porch. I just carried them in the back door and dropped them on the floor in the kitchen and in the bedroom.

The minute we walked in, Kara called her friend Susan and told her we had come back early. Susan had wanted Kara to come over and spend the day at her pool on Sunday, but Kara had told her we would be out of town. She woke Susan up and told her we were back. Susan said she would come get Kara about 7:00 a.m. She did come and honked her horn for Kara. They drove away to spend the day at Susan's apartment/pool that day.

That was why I was alone when the man began beating on my den door and told me "Mister, your barn's on fire." My stressful weekend was about to get even worse. I had driven almost one thousand miles, missed our friends in Birmingham, and missed our friends in Kentucky, and the worst part of the weekend was still to come. We really had no idea.

CHAPTER 3

THE RENTED PROPERTY

July 13, 1997, was one of those typical Memphis summer days that was so hot and humid it seemed as if the trees themselves were sweating even at 8:28 a.m.

We lived in a little prefabricated three-bedroom house. It set on a beautiful piece of property. The property was just outside the city limits of Bartlett, Tennessee, in Shelby County. There was a four-lane divided highway that ran in front of the property when we moved in. When a new mall began going in about a mile away, the highway was expanded to six lanes, with a large shoulder area on each side. Over fifty-nine thousand cars passed up and down that highway every day.

The house itself faced north, toward the highway. It sat upon an elevated area about fifty feet off the highway. It had a deep ditch in front of the house. There was a gravel driveway that crossed the ditch on each side of the property, circled up in front of the house (uphill), then ran downhill and back across the ditch. The little house was on eight acres of land. At least six of those acres were covered by old hardwood timber. Trees stretching up more than fifty feet high covered the property except the backyard. Even the front yard had some one-thousand-year-old trees, providing shade in front of the house. The backyard was surrounded by the large trees, and it too was shaded much of the day.

To the west of the little house, there was a large slab of concrete. Apparently, the original farmhouse had set on that slab of concrete. The old barn set even farther west than the concrete slab. The edge of the woods was right up against the barn on its west side.

It was a beautiful piece of property especially in the summer, with all the trees in full greenery. A real estate company owned the property. There was a For Sale sign in the front yard. The property had been zoned as commercial. The real estate agent said when they sold the property, they would move the little house. We had an option to buy the house or move into it after it was moved and continue to rent it.

To the west of the property beyond the woods about a mile away was a landscaping nursery business. There was nothing else in that direction except a quick shop and then a side street called Appling Road. On the other side of the house, there was a large section of woods where three radio/TV towers were located. Beyond the woods was Kate Bond Road. After that, a series of car dealerships and other businesses.

It was nice to sit in the shady front yard early in the morning and drink a cup of coffee and read the paper and just watch the traffic pass by on the busy highway. It was quiet, peaceful, and serene. The only home on the other side of the six-lane highway sat right across the road. It was an old country farmhouse with a barn and farm equipment scattered all around on about three hundred acres of farmland. It wasn't uncommon for the state highway patrol to set up speed traps in front of either of our houses.

I once heard the older woman that lived across the highway had been offered $8 million for her property, but she refused to sell. She wanted to keep the family farm.

To the best of my knowledge, the old farmhouse and farmland are still there and still belong to the same family. Despite repeated efforts, the old lady refused to sell regardless of the amount. I don't know what happened to the house we lived in. I am told there is now a large car dealership located on that piece of property and the beautiful old trees are now all gone. However, on July 13, 1997, the house, barn, and woods were still standing.

CHAPTER 4

THE FIRE DEPARTMENT

The heat coming from the fire was amazing. I was only wearing a T-shirt that said NCAA Final Four 1984, a pair of thin gym shorts, and flip-flop sandals, but I was covered in sweat. All I had been doing was holding two water hoses together and trying to spray the water on the roof where I could see the flames. I was losing that battle. The fire was growing second by second.

The fire trucks began arriving. They had trouble parking their large vehicles. A dozen or so cars had pulled over in front of the house, and several local county police cars had pulled into the driveway, so there was very little room for the pumper trucks or water trucks belonging to the fire department. The fire hydrant was just east of the driveway on the east side of the property. They hooked their hoses up to the hydrant and the water pumper trucks they had brought with them. They dragged the heavy hoses across the yard and prepared to fight the fire.

They yelled at me to "put the hoses down and get out of the way." I laid them down and moved them back toward the house. I went around the back of the house and turned off the faucet and then went to the front of the house and turned off that faucet. The firemen sprung into action.

I noticed several of them putting on oxygen tanks, masks, and other protective equipment. It was obvious they were going to fight the fire from the inside as well as the outside of the structure. They were extremely well coordinated and professional as they went about their business. It was all done in a very businesslike manner.

My dad had been a volunteer fireman my entire life. He worked for the local utility company and, naturally, served on the volunteer fire department. It had always been his job to cut the utilities to a structure on fire. I had been to a number of fires with him over the years. I had great respect and admiration for firemen and all they did in the course of doing their job.

The only thing I said to the firemen that morning was to warn them about the stairs to the upper floor located in the back of the barn. The homemade stairs were very, very narrow. In looking at the boots the firemen were wearing and all the gear they had and considering the smoke and heat, I didn't see how any of them could actually climb those particular stairs. They thanked me and assured me they would be careful.

With that said and done, I went into the house and watched the firemen work from the safety of my house. Within twenty minutes (I would say by around 9:15 a.m.), they had the flames at least all knocked down. There had been and still was a tremendous amount of smoke, but the fire itself was out. I looked over at the television, which was on, and was surprised to see just how much smoke there was coming from the old barn. One of the TV stations had a helicopter in the air, providing a live shot. The smoke just seemed to rise from among the tall trees on the property.

The crowd out front grew too. By now there were upward of fifty people milling around in the large front yard—curious citizens, firemen, and local police. I was finally cooling off as the air conditioner hummed in the house.

Eventually, I guess about 9:30 a.m., a fire marshal and his assistant knocked on my front door. I let them in. They were extremely cordial and asked me if I knew anything about the fire or its cause. I explained that I had been out of town and only arrived back at home around 3:00 a.m. I told them how I was awakened by a bicyclist pounding on my front door, telling me the building was on fire. I told them I had grabbed a phone, dialed 911, and handed it to the bicyclist with instructions to report the fire. They wanted to know if I was the only one there. I told them I was and that my wife had left the residence with a friend an hour or more before the fire was reported to me. They thanked me and left.

CHAPTER 5

THE CROWD CHANGES

The people who had originally stopped to watch the fire were leaving. The fire marshal left, and the firemen began taking off their gear and preparing to withdraw. Only a fraction remained to work the fire site. It was basically just smoldering now. The gravel driveway and most of the yard was covered in water, filled with soot and ash. The Sheetrock had come loose and fallen from the ceiling of the bottom floor from the weight of the water that had been sprayed on the fire upstairs. The old hot tub we had in the garage was filled with the dirty black water and some pieces of Sheetrock. Everything else was soaked and dripping. There was nothing of any value left in the old barn, but if there had been, it would have all been ruined by the fire or water.

I noticed that several different-looking vehicles began pulling into the driveway and parking right in front of the house. Most of the vehicles seemed to be Broncos, Blazers, Pathfinders, or some other kind of utility SUV-type vehicles. The men getting out of these vehicles were also noticeable. Most had guns strapped to their belts. They were wearing blue jeans and everyday clothes (even T-shirts). The guns had a profound effect on me. They looked much different than any of the other people that had been there that day. I had an extremely uneasy feeling standing there in my house and looking at this group that had just arrived.

I did two things. First, I called my brother, Paul. I had meant to call him earlier when I realized he might see the smoke from the fire on TV and be really worried, but I had never made the call. Local television vans and trucks had also arrived and were parked along the highway on both sides of the road. Paul did not answer his phone, so I left a voice message. I looked at the clock. It was near 10:00 a.m. on Sunday morning, and I knew he would be at church. I told him on the message the old barn was on fire and not the house. I told him we were fine, but I wanted him to call me. Secondly, I called my wife at Susan's to tell her about the fire. I was lucky to catch her and Susan back at the apartment. They had just come back from the pool area to use the bathroom and get something to drink. While I was talking with her, my call waiting received another call. I told her to wait. It was a friend of mine who had seen the television reports. He wanted to know if we were all right. He had lived at my house previously with us but had gone back to Missouri. He was in town putting a motor in a truck for a friend who owned a pallet company. He asked if there was anything he could do. I gave him Susan's phone number and told him to call, get directions, and then go by and get Kara and bring her home. He assured me he would. I hung up and told Kara he would be calling and I would feel better if she came back home. She got to the house about thirty minutes later (around 10:30 a.m.).

Meanwhile, I continued to watch the new men outside my home. The firemen left, but the crowd of new men grew larger. They began going in and out of the old barn. They seemed to be grouping up into small groups, talking quietly. They would point toward the barn and then toward the house. They were walking around my dad's car and actually looking inside the car, which was parked in the front eastern area of the house. I had borrowed my dad's car earlier because mine had been in the shop and I continued having electrical problems. They were also looking at my 1995 Camaro the same way. It was parked behind the house.

When Kara got home, I caught her up on all the events. We watched the new men walk all over the property. They were going into the woods and looking into a couple of little pump houses out back. They were making me nervous. I didn't know why. It was just one of those moments when a person knows something is not quite right. I went to the telephone and tried to call my brother again. I left him another message and told him there were some strange men going all over the property and even looking in our cars. I told him something wasn't right and asked him to call me as soon as he could.

Little did I know just how wrong things really were. Paul wouldn't check his phone messages until after five o'clock that day. Our lives would be radically changed by then.

CHAPTER 6

INVADED

At some time that morning, our house was invaded. One minute we were alone in the house, looking out the window and watching all the activity. The next moment, men and women were pouring into our home. We had been invaded.

Right before we were invaded, I remember seeing what looked like a large silver ball slightly larger than a basketball. This silver ball was carried from the smoldering barn and laid on the slab of concrete where the old farmhouse must have sat. This silver ball looked heavy. I assumed it was solid but had no idea what it was. It certainly grew a crowd of people. It was quite fascinating. Eight to ten curious people crowded around it. They seemed as curious as I was as to what it was. I called Kara over to the window on the west side of the house. I said, "Kara, look at that."

She replied, "Wow! What is that?"

I answered, "I have no idea."

They finally rolled the ball around and around but seemed just as mystified. Finally, one of the men showed up with a large ax. They began whacking at the ball. It wasn't long before he penetrated the stubborn shell, but we would not see the end of the encounter. It was at that moment that men and women began pouring into our house through the front and back doors. Some were police officers in uniform. Others wore just plain clothes.

The group fanned out and began to browse throughout the house. I heard closet doors opening and closing and drawers being opened and slammed shut. They created quite a commotion. We stepped from the kitchen into the living room / den area and were confronted by a plain-clothed large man with long hair. He had a gun on the right side of his belt and a badge on the left side. He identified himself as Detective Martin.

He told us to sit down and then asked us, "What's going on here?"

I said, "That's exactly what we would like to know. What are all of you doing in our house, going through everything?"

He said, "What's your name?"

I told him I was Jack Phillips and my wife was Kara Phillips.

He asked us, "Do you live here?"

I said, "Yes, we do."

He told me we both might be in trouble. He said it looked like a crime had been committed in the barn.

I asked, "What kind of crime?"

All he said was "We'll get to that later. You two just sit here."

Naturally, our apprehension was ratcheted up 100 percent. I had already felt that small dread earlier, but I did feel better now that Kara was home. I thought about Paul and wished my older brother would call. I couldn't say Kara felt the same way I did. I know she sensed my uneasiness. She had continually been asking me "Jack, what's wrong?" or "What's wrong? You're acting funny." I had just brushed her off because I really wasn't sure what was wrong. Now, as our house had been invaded and was currently being thoroughly searched—from bathroom to bedroom—I was disturbed and frankly getting pissed off.

Detective Martin came in with another man. He said, "Mr. Phillips, this is Special Agent March." I nodded at the guy and noticed he had a gun on his belt but no badge. He didn't look like any agent I had ever seen, and I wondered what kind of agent he was. Detective Martin said Agent March would like to talk. I said, "Let's talk then."

He asked me to come into the kitchen. I did, and we sat down at the kitchen table. He pulled out a small tape recorder and said, "Mind if we record this?"

I said, "No, I don't mind at all."

He began asking general background questions about me and Kara, our jobs, our trips, and a variety of other seemingly unrelated, meaningless questions. I think at some point he read me my rights and then turned the tape recorder on. I noticed that people continued to enter and leave the house by the front door and the back door. I saw two women officers, both in uniform, walk down the hall with Kara. They all three went into the bathroom.

I still just had on the T-shirt and thin gym shorts. All Kara was wearing was a two-piece bathing suit covered by a T-shirt and some cutoff jeans. Both doors to the house were standing wide open, and the air conditioner was running full throttle. It was hot outside. I was sweating from nerves and shivering because I was really cold from the air conditioning.

I noticed a Shelby Count officer, whom I would later learn was Sergeant Earnest Lewis, the ranking Shelby County officer on the scene. He was in the den, snapping off pictures. Then he came through the kitchen and went into the utility room. He began taking photographs in there too. *Snap snap snap*, I heard the camera click. He then seemed to be going room to room, taking more pictures. There was a steady stream of people going in and out of the house, maybe as many as twenty.

Kara returned down the hall from the bathroom with the two female officers right behind her. It seemed they were headed back into the den. Kara looked at me as she passed, and for the first time, I saw pure terror on her face and in her eyes! I don't think I had ever seen such pure fear or such intensity in her eyes. We had been married twenty-seven years, with a three-year courtship before that. I had seen her afraid when she was in labor giving birth to our two children, but I had never seen her terrified. That was what I saw at that moment. I would find out later that she had been totally strip-searched by the two female officers. This was the first time she had experienced that indignity. I had never experienced that.

The conversation with Martin and March became an interrogation at some point. And I was about to find out what that strange-looking silver ball was and what was in it.

CHAPTER 7

INTERROGATED
AND IMPRISONED

Detective Martin became aggressive. He and Agent March began playing the "good cop, bad cop" routine with me. Eventually, they gave that up, and both became aggressive. I felt like they were trying to intimidate me. They challenged everything I said. They repeatedly called me a liar. They tried to trip me up by asking for the same information in a myriad of ways with camouflaged questions.

The tape recorder was humming. I asked them if I could retrieve my billfold off the television in the living room / den. They let me do that, and I grabbed the billfold and some credit card receipts off the TV. I explained I had been in room 206 of the Days' Inn in Fultondale, Alabama, all weekend, and I showed them my receipt, which showed I had checked out on Saturday, July 12, at 11:55 a.m. I showed them Exxon credit card receipts that were stamped with dates and times. It was easy to trace our journey through Nashville to Oak Grove, Kentucky. Then the night of the twelfth and early morning hours of the thirteenth, it was easy to trace our trip back through Nashville and then to Memphis. We had been of town—it was obvious. Everything we bought, we had purchased with a credit card, and it was all documented on those credit card receipts. Each receipt showed not only where we were located but also the times and dates. Our timeline was right there for them to see in black and white.

The crowd in the house had thinned out, although some officers still prowled around. Sergeant Lewis with the camera and his crew had left the house, at least. I found out that the agent at the table with me was Drug Enforcement Agent (DEA) Mike March. I assure you, there was nothing special about Agent March. He had been identified to me at some point as Special Agent March.

Agent March could best be described as slimy looking. His hair was greasy and so was his skin. His hair was combed back, and he looked like a wannabe mafia figure. There didn't seem to be a live spark in his eyes. Maybe his eyes had seen too much of the inhumanity of man. Maybe he had been in the business too long already. Whatever the reason, he gave off an aura of being too close to the dark side. I am not describing him in a moral sense. No, not at all. He just appeared almost lifeless, dark, and slimy in the physical sense.

Although I couldn't see a clock from where I sat, I knew it had to be between 12:30 p.m. and 1:00 p.m. At some point, either Detective Martin or Agent March asked me a question—I can't recall the specific question—that was obviously loaded. It flashed through my mind that if I answered in a positive way, they could use my answer and make me look guilty. At the same time, if I answered in a negative way, they could twist that answer and make me appear just as guilty. I had a revelation. They really thought the burned-up meth lab they had found in the barn was mine, or ours. That both shook me up and surprised me. They had just dropped the fact of the existence of the meth lab on me. That was surprising enough. But for them to think we were involved, that was ridiculous. I had shown them where we had been. I was a schoolteacher and a coach, for God's sake. Didn't they realize I was a finalist for teacher of the year for the second straight year? That is, I was one of the five finalists out of twenty-four thousand teachers in Shelby County for the second year in a row. Didn't they realize I didn't do drugs or even know how to manufacture meth? Did they really suspect us? Did they not realize my brother and I had helped to start the Fellowship of Christian Athletes in Memphis over twenty years before? Did they not realize that I worked (for free) at Memphis State University in their summer antidrug program for athletes every year? Did they not know I had been taking people into our home with drug and alcohol problems and helping them for the last two years? Could they really suspect us?

I was forty-seven years old. I had four grandchildren. Did they really think I would be involved with making or manufacturing any drug? Didn't they realize I had no money or possessions that would indicated drug involvement? Didn't they realize my wife worked at Walmart, and we lived paycheck to paycheck? Didn't they know I rented a house because we could not afford to buy? Didn't they know we had never been in trouble or been arrested for anything—ever? Didn't they know my dad was an ordained minister? Didn't they know I had spent half my adult life teaching and coaching, and much of it in private Christian schools? Didn't our life matter? Didn't a lifetime of contributing to society and helping others matter? I had a college degree (BS) and a master's degree (MA) in secondary education administration and supervision. Didn't they know that I knew better than to commit such a crime? Now, they've asked me a loaded question. I realized they really wanted to charge Kara and me.

I refused to answer the question and told them I wanted an attorney before I would say anything else. They turned off the tape recorder and, after cursing me for a few minutes, showed me the cost of exercising my constitutional right to an attorney.

Agent March called in a fifty-something-year-old Shelby County deputy and ordered him to handcuff me, take me to the den, handcuff my wife, and guard us. His instructions were, "If they so much as move, shoot them." It was our first time to ever be handcuffed. I was shoved down into my recliner. I told the officer, "The handcuffs are way too tight. This will not work. I have a dead nerve in my left shoulder and a torn rotator cuff in my right shoulder. With my arms behind me, both shoulders are already throbbing and killing me." He just stared at me. My hands and shoulders were already throbbing.

Kara sat in her chair, weeping. She looked up at me and said, "Jack, what's going on? What have we done to deserve this? Why are they doing this to us?" Three questions. Three questions I could not answer that day. Three questions I still can't answer.

Detective Martin and his partner whispered in the hallway. They conferred with Agent March, and we watched out the picture window of our home as Detective Martin and his partner climbed into a Ford Bronco and drove away. Agent March and his buddies continued to dig through our possessions, searching here and there. The deputy guarding us just sat across the room and stared at us.

We were both freezing cold and only half-dressed. The morning had started off clear, hot, muggy, and sunny. Then during my interrogation, clouds had come up, and sometime between 12:00 p.m. and 12:30 p.m., a summer thunderstorm had developed. By 1:00 p.m., there was thunder and lightning and pouring rain. It was as hard a summer rain as we had seen the entire season. We both watched it rain and storm out the window.

Suddenly, I focused on the large cardboard box sitting in my front yard under a tree. The track uniforms. They were barely a month old. There was no need for them to sit under that tree and get soaked and wet and then mildew.

I asked the officer, "Sir, can I go out and get those track uniforms in that box under the tree? Or will you go get them? There is no reason for those uniforms to be ruined by sitting out under that tree in the rain. The kids at school certainly had nothing to do with this."

He looked at me, paused a moment, and then hollered for Agent March. March came down the hall into the den and said, "Yeah?"

He told him, "He wants to go out and get that box. He said it had some kind of school uniforms in it and he didn't want them to get ruined setting out in the rain."

March stood there a minute and said, "Okay, unhandcuff him and let him get the uniforms. But if he tries to do anything else, shoot him in the back."

The officer came over, stood me up, and took the handcuffs off. My shoulders were completely numb. We walked toward the door and stopped as we got there. He turned around and looked me straight in the eyes. He said, "If you run, motherfucker, I'll shoot you in the back. Do you understand?" With that, he opened the door with one hand and pulled out his service revolver with the other.

I said, "I understand." I went out and grabbed the box of uniforms. I brought them in and sat them right in the middle of the den. The officer handcuffed me again and placed me in my chair. I was now wet and colder than before. The back door was still standing wide open. The air conditioner had not stopped running all day.

Kara asked to go the bathroom, so Agent March and a female officer came and escorted her down the hall. They took her handcuffs off, and she and the female officer both went into the bathroom. When they came out of the bathroom, Agent March and another male officer took Kara into our bedroom. I found out from Kara later that they questioned her about the meth lab. Of course, she was clueless. They grilled her for more than fifteen minutes. They never read her her Miranda rights. She didn't say anything incriminating because she didn't know anything incriminating. She told them the same things I had told them. The point is, they violated her constitutional rights without pause or thought. They returned her to the den, reapplied the handcuffs, and placed her in the other chair.

Time passed slowly. It was still early midafternoon. I had had nothing to eat or drink that whole day. I was handcuffed in my own house and had two numb and aching shoulders. Now I had to go to the bathroom. It was a bathroom need you usually get when you are extremely nervous. I asked the officer if I could go.

Again, he called for Agent March and told him, "He needs to go to the bathroom. Can I let him go?"

March looked at me and said, "I can't talk to him. He asked for a lawyer."

I told him, "If you don't let me go, I'm going to crap all over myself and this chair."

March looked down at the officer and said, "Would you tell him I don't hear him? I can't talk to him because he lawyered up." He walked off down the hall.

I shouted at his back, "I'll talk to you without a lawyer. I have nothing to hide. You just can't ask me loaded questions and expect me to answer them so you can use whatever I say against me and make me look guilty. I am not stupid. I was talking to you before, and I will talk to you again, but I have to go to the bathroom now!"

He turned around and told the officer, "Let him go."

I went to the bathroom and made it just in time. I must have been 2:00 p.m. or so. When I came back, they hooked the handcuffs back on me, but this time, they put me in a chair at the kitchen table. Out came the tape recorder again. They had two different people read me my Miranda rights, explaining that I had now agreed to talk again without a lawyer of my own free will. The interrogation began again.

At 2:41 p.m., a lady officer in plain clothes began videotaping everything. She started outside the house under an umbrella. The time she recorded was on the videotape she made. There was another officer with her, making a new set of photographs. She was talking and giving a running commentary on what she was filming. I saw her open the doors to my car and my dad's car and videotaped inside and outside the cars.

She then entered the house and continued her videotaping with a running monologue while the other officers snapped off picture after picture. There were six or seven clocks scattered around our house in the various rooms. She captured me writhing on the floor in front of my recliner with my hands cuffed behind my back. I had slid off into the floor trying to get some relief. I had turned sideways and was leaning against the recliner, trying to relieve some of the pain in my shoulders. She videotaped in the kitchen, the utility room, and the three bedrooms. We would later discover they had tossed every drawer in every dresser and every closet in the house. There were now two sets of still photographs: one from the morning, when the sun was shining and it was bright and clear, and one from the afternoon, when it was pouring down rain and cloudy, as well as a videotape. She got into my car and videotaped it just like she had my dad's car. The other officer continued to take still photos as well. They took pictures and videotaped the barn, the woods, and all around the house on the outside.

At about 3:15 p.m., Detective Martin and his partner returned. He came in the front door and showed me a search warrant. He laid it on the end table next to my shoulder. My first thought was, *That's a little bit late*. Later, I would learn the search warrant had been signed at two forty-one at a general sessions court judge's house. This judge, Judge Chriss, had his Sunday afternoon at home interrupted by the two detectives. His home was more than a thirty-five-minute drive from my residence on a sunny day. It was still storming that Sunday afternoon. The National Weather Service would later report it began raining between 12:00 p.m. and 12:30 p.m. that day and continued raining (at least on the half hour when they reported) until almost 7:00 p.m. that night. It rained 1.36 inches that afternoon.

My home had been invaded and searched illegally for hours. We had been held captive, literally handcuffed, for hours upon hours when we were *not* under arrest. We had been cursed and twice threatened with being shot in the back. My wife had been strip-searched in our own home and illegally questioned. I had been denied a lawyer even after I asked for one and then made to talk without one by being denied use of my own bathroom. I had been insulted and disrespected.

At about 3:30 p.m., Agent March came into the living room / den area holding something in his hand. That something was wrapped in duct tape. There was some kind of plastic wrapping under the duct tape. He told me he had taken this object from the silver ball that turned out to be what was left of a small fire safe. The silver ball was all that was left of the fire safe. The rest of it had melted away.

He had gloves on and said, "It looks like we have a kilo of cocaine here. We should be able to get some fingerprints off this duct tape."

I told him, "Good. I don't own a safe nor have I ever seen a safe. Whatever that is, it isn't mine. You won't find my fingerprints or Kara's fingerprints on that or anything else in there."

He told me an officer was getting his kit so he could test it to see exactly what it was. He began unwrapping it, and I noticed there was more duct tape and more plastic underneath the duct tape and plastic wrapping I had seen before. In fact, there were about three layers of each. It was really wrapped up.

They went into the kitchen and set up their test kit to test the block.

We only had a small countertop to the left of the double sink. That was where they set up the test kit. Although I couldn't see them,

I could hear them talking. It seemed they scraped just a small sliver off the bar and that an even smaller piece from the sliver fell into the sink. Whatever happened, there was a tremendous explosion. There was an open archway between the kitchen and our living room / den area, where we were. A great blue ball of flame shot across our living room/ den. Kara and I both ducked for safety. It blew up their test kit.

As it turned out, it wasn't cocaine at all or any other drug. I learned later it was sodium metal. It is used in industrial settings and is extremely volatile when it comes in contact with any kind of water. It is a highly regulated product, and only licensed and registered consumers can buy it. I have been told that every bar is etched with a serial number so it can be easily tracked. There was probably enough there to level the barn and the house and leave a large crater. It was frightening to realize how much water the fire department had sprayed on the fire. I would suspect it was hundreds of thousands of gallons of water. Thank God the sodium metal was in that silver ball (the fire safe). If not, this story would have ended that day.

However, it was just beginning. During the course of my second interrogation, they had asked if I would take a lie detector test. I was hesitant. I had a friend that was a police officer in St. Louis, Missouri. He had told me how he had been trained to manipulate the breath intoxication machine to make it read that anyone he tested was intoxicated. That flashed through my mind. I wondered if they could do the same with the lie detector machine.

However, I found myself saying "Okay, I'll take the lie detector test without a lawyer with a few qualifications. First, no one touches the machine while I am being tested. Secondly, you only ask me about using or manufacturing meth. I'll answer any and all questions about that. You can ask me if I know how to manufacture meth, if I ever have manufactured meth, and if I was manufacturing meth in that old barn. There's the phone. Call the lie detector person and let's do it." I was never asked about or given a lie detector test. I assure you, if given such a test today, I could still pass.

I had also been told there was a large metal cabinet/desk in the burned-up lab upstairs in the old barn. They told me it was full of tools. They said neither the fire nor the water had touched those tools. They threatened me by saying they were going to take finger-prints off all those tools.

I was delighted! My dad, who worked with tools everyday as an electrician, would never let my brother or me use any tools. We are the most inept men with tools around. I probably had a screw-driver and maybe one of my dad's lock wrenches in a junk drawer in the kitchen. That would be the extent of my tools. I knew the tools they were talking about didn't belong to me. I also knew the metal cabinet/desk wasn't mine. I told them, "If you take the fingerprints, you will find out who was manufacturing meth in that barn, and it won't be me."

The officers miraculously pulled out one more piece of evi-dence out of the upstairs fire scene. It was late in the afternoon, after 5:00 p.m., and the rain had let up for a moment. I had asked the question in the second interview, "How do you know it was a func-tioning meth lab? The wiring in the old barn was shot. How do you know that a meth lab was in operation and had anything to do with the fire?"

It was that question I believe that prompted the new discovery. One of the Shelby County deputies and Agent March came out of the barn carrying a plain plastic mop bucket. We could see them out the window. The old mop bucket was a cheap, ordinary flesh-colored mop bucket with a wire handle. I knew it was a mop bucket because I had seen it in a trash pile in the woods weeks before the fire.

However, it was now being claimed that the old mop bucket was found upstairs and had survived the fire and that it contained sixty-five grams of meth. That would prove it was a functioning meth lab. I'll come back to the bucket later. The officer proudly posed for pictures with the new find.

At about 6:30 or 7:00 p.m., my brother Paul showed up. Was I glad to see him! I heard him ask one of the detectives "What's going on here?" The detective told him the barn had burned and a meth lab had been found in the burned-up barn (upstairs). Paul asked him if we were under arrest. The detective said, "No." When Paul came in and saw we were handcuffed, he told them to uncuff us and let us go if we weren't under arrest. They immediately released us. We had been handcuffed for almost seven hours.

By 7:15 p.m., we were all alone—me, Kara, and Paul. I immediately told him we didn't know anything about it and had nothing to do with it.

He knew we had been out of town. I told him the events of the preceding days and how we had just gotten home in the early hours and were now at this point. He looked at me and said, "Jack, that's good enough for me. I believe you."

He meant it too. He knew I would never lie to him. Him believing in me at that moment meant so much to both Kara and me. I knew it wouldn't matter to Paul if we were guilty or not. He would support us either way. His trust and confidence in me said a lot about our relationship. I would never lie to him, and I wasn't lying this time.

Paul left about 8:30 p.m. Kara and I looked at each other, hugged each other, and cried a lot. We walked through our house knee-deep in clothes and personal possessions. The file cabinet had even been emptied, and all its papers were scattered in two rooms. The desk, dressers, chests, and closets had all been ransacked. Our shoes were even buried under the avalanche of clothing. All our personal papers had just been tossed about. Our lives were scattered everywhere on the floor. We dug out a path to the bedroom and went to sleep holding each other. It had been a long, long, tough five days. The last twelve hours had been brutal, unlike anything we had ever experienced or ever even imagined.

CHAPTER 8

THE NEXT THREE DAYS

Monday, July 14, was a tough day for Kara and me. We were both up by 5:00 a.m. We had barely slept. On our way to bed, we had literally made a path through the living room / den, down the hall, and across the bedroom to bed.

Now, we faced the daunting task of putting everything back in its place. I had another problem as well. We were supposed to go pick up the two oldest grandchildren to come spend the week with us. Since we had come home early Sunday morning instead of Tuesday night as we planned, we decided to try to go to Rector on Tuesday and stay all night there, pick up the grandchildren, and return to Memphis on Wednesday. We had to get the house back in order before we left. We couldn't bring the grandchildren home to this mess. Our Monday was laid out in front of us literally, covering most of the floor space in our entire house.

It was astonishing how tired and drained we were. The last twenty-four hours had taken a tremendous physical, mental, and emotional toll on us. We fixed a pot of coffee, sat in the same chairs we were in the day before (without the handcuffs), opened the blinds, and watched another day dawn.

Some time that morning, we called Mary Lynn and told her of our plans to come on Tuesday, pick up the children, and return to Memphis on Wednesday. Everyone thought it was a good idea. We also called the DEA office number we had been given. They had told us to try to make a list of anyone we knew who had a motorcycle. We didn't know why. We quickly made up a list of about six or seven individuals, including my dad. We told them we would be leaving town later that week and would drop off the list.

After working most of the morning, Kara went to McDonald's and grabbed a couple of burgers for lunch. We didn't have much of an appetite. We worked pretty well straight through, and by 3:00 p.m., we had everything in its place.

I wished the sun had already set because that old burned-out barn sat there like a fresh wound. Every time I looked at it, I felt the anguish from the day before all over again. The barn was like an ugly scar on the landscape of the beautiful piece of property. I felt a continuous reminder of the fear, anxiety, humiliation, and exhaustion from what we had been through. The small dread I had felt as the strangers arrived on the property during the fire had morphed into full-blown stress and anxiety for both of us. We had kept the blinds closed most of that day. Also, the phone had not rung once the entire day.

We needed to get out of the house and get away from there. We had not planned on leaving until Tuesday, but we decided to pack our bags, drop by the DEA office and drop off the list, and just check into a motel room out of town. It was like we had a malignancy that no one wanted to be around.

We packed a few things and headed north after stopping off at the DEA office. They had only a few minimal questions for us. We ended up in Blytheville, Arkansas, and checked into a Holiday Inn there. We took a shower and planned on watching TV.

On the way, the car had acted up again. We actually had to stop once at a rest stop and turn the car off to let the battery recharge. Since we had already showered at the motel and it was still early evening and daylight, I had an idea.

I told Kara, "Let's go get something to eat. How about we call Timmy and Donna and run over to their house and see if Timmy will look at this car?" She thought it was a great idea, so she called Donna.

Donna told Kara that Timmy wasn't home at the moment but would be back anytime and for us to come on over. She gave us directions to their new farmhouse near Campbell, Missouri. They had previously lived outside of Caruthersville, Missouri. We had gone to that house once because they had some furniture they were throwing away. We had never been to their new residence.

We drove over and found the house on the eleven-acre farm without any trouble. Timmy was not home, but there was still some daylight left. Donna seemed really glad to see us. We told her the whole story about the fire and everything that had transpired the week before and the day of the fire. Timmy eventually showed up on a brand-new, shiny black motorcycle. It was beautiful. He had just purchased it that afternoon. I knew he had wrecked his old motorcycle when he injured his leg. I guessed this was his replacement motorcycle. He worked on the car, and I told him all about the fire and all the things we had just told Donna. As we were just preparing to go back to the motel, a guy named Sam Nance pulled up on a new black motorcycle just like Timmy's. They said they had purchased them at the same place at the same time. They were really nice bikes. I was envious.

I had not moved to Memphis until 1975. While in Rector, I had umpired Little League baseball games. Sam Nance had been a nine-year-old player when I moved away. I had not seen him again until 1994. I was in my car with a friend at a stop sign. Someone pulled up opposite me at the four-way stop. The person in the other vehicle (a Jeep) was waving like crazy. My friend told me that was Sam Nance. He said Sam had been away in the navy. I would have never recognized him.

I told Sam the whole story about the fire. That was the third time I had told the story that night. We left their house about 11:30 p.m. and made the trip back to the motel in Blytheville. We were still tired and had frayed nerves, but we actually got a pretty good night's sleep. At least my car was running better even though it wasn't quite right.

The next day, we got to Rector, and a friend of mine took me to the auto parts store, and I purchased a new alternator. He installed it for me. We stayed in Rector at my parents' house Tuesday night then picked up the grandchildren and returned to Memphis on the sixteenth.

CHAPTER 9

HOME WITH THE GRANDKIDS

The days flew by with the grandchildren there. What a delight! They were just what we needed. Our eldest granddaughter was eight years old. Her little brother was five. They were wonderful children. They never asked for anything, and we never had to tell them twice to do something.

We played ball in the backyard, went to the zoo, spent a lot of time at McDonald's, rented and watched movies, and did whatever we could come up with so they would have fun. Kara and I were still haunted by that old burned-up barn just sitting there. The children were fascinated by it, but I think they sensed we really didn't want to talk much about it.

Two significant things occurred that week. First, on Thursday, July 17, the real estate agent that owned the property called and said he would come by Friday to look at the property. He said he wanted to make arrangements to clean up that mess as soon as he could. He couldn't do it fast enough for us. Secondly, on Friday, he did come by. He was very cordial to us and said he would try to have a crew there to clean up the mess on Monday, July 21. We made a decision right then to be out of town when that occurred. If we took the children home on the twenty-first, we could just stay in Rector a few days and then come back to Memphis.

I also had an idea: that it might be to our advantage to set up a blood drug screen test. I told Kara my idea and added that if anyone accused us again, at least we would have a clean drug screen. We looked in the yellow pages and found a doctor that gave such tests. We called and made an appointment for the twenty-third (Wednesday). It was going to cost thirty-five dollars a piece (seventy dollars), and we didn't have the money. I would be paid by direct deposit on Monday. We wanted to be out of town Monday and Tuesday, so Wednesday made the most sense. We made the appointment.

The weekend passed, and we headed to Rector on Monday, the twenty-first, as planned. We played with the newborn and the rest of the children. We visited both our families and had a relaxing weekend.

Tuesday night, July 22, about 6:00 p.m., my mother was cutting my hair in her beauty shop in her home. She had moved the beauty shop there when her partner and sister passed away about ten years before. She had been a licensed beautician for over forty years. In her beauty shop, she had a television. Rector, Arkansas, picked up the CBS affiliate out of Cape Girardeau, Missouri (channel 12). One of the stories on the local news certainly grabbed my attention.

As my mom cut my hair and we talked, I looked up at the television. The entire screen was a head shot of one man. It was my friend, Timmy Tisdale. There was his picture with his name transposed on the screen: Timmy Tisdale.

I told my mom, "I know that guy. Turn it up, Mom." Just as she reached to turn it up, another face popped up on the entire screen. It was a head shot of Sam Nance. It too was captioned with his name.

The announcer was telling about a big DEA drug bust at a house just outside of Cape Girardeau, Missouri. They showed a picture of a nice brick home on a hill. According to the report, the men in that house were cooking meth. They showed about six other men with small head shots on the same screen and said they were involved too. They reported that Nance and Tisdale were arrested with the other six men. I thought of Donna. I knew she would be crushed. The report said the DEA had infiltrated their group with an undercover agent months before. The report said the cook had started three days

before on the nineteenth of July, and the DEA, the SEMO Drug
Task Force, the Cape County Sheriff's Department, and others had
surrounded the house and watched them cooking (going in and out
of the house with supplies) for three days. It said Nance had run out
the back door carrying a nine-millimeter pistol and had been struck
on the head and disarmed. There were no shots fired. They were all
being held in the county jail in Perryville, Missouri.

I was stunned! Could it be? Could these men have been involved
in the lab fire in the old barn on the property where I lived? Memphis
was two hundred miles from Cape Girardeau. Would they have gone
there to cook so soon after the fire in Memphis? Also, I had just seen
both of them on the fifteenth at Timmy and Donna's house. Could
they have kept a straight face while I told them my story and not
given it away? Were they that coldhearted? Surely not! Also, Timmy
had a hole in his leg. I had seen it myself on July 8. He could barely
walk. He certainly could not have climbed those narrow stairs on
that leg. No. They couldn't have been involved. True, they did own
motorcycles, and I had given their names to the DEA. The motorcycles they had owned were white. Their new ones were black. But still,
this had been an ongoing thing in Missouri. They had a DEA agent
in their group. He would have known it if they had caused the fire,
and he would have reported it, and they would have been arrested
for it.

I guess I was trying to rationalize it away. I did not want to
think they would leave me in that house asleep while all that water
was being sprayed on the fire and that sodium metal right there.
Also, the house could easily have caught fire. They wouldn't have left
me asleep, would they? No, they had no reason to be at my house.
Obviously, they had been cooking all over Missouri. It was a long
jump to Memphis from Cape Girardeau.

Chapter 10

HOME AND ANOTHER
SCHOOL YEAR

We made our blood test appointment on the twenty-third. The nurse told us they would call us and have the results in about a week. Kara had taken a leave of absence from Walmart, but she returned to part-time work on the twenty-eighth. I had in-service training beginning on the twenty-eighth. The new school year was underway.

I worked at one of the largest high schools in the state of Tennessee. We had about 2,300 students in high school. My classroom was actually one of three industrial/vocational classrooms. It was upstairs and had a window that looked down directly into the bay in the auto shop department. Noise, at first, from the garage was a problem. However, I had grown use to it, and so did all my social study students.

The doctor's office called our house on July 29 and told us our test results could be picked up the next day. Kara was off that day, so when I got home from school about 2:40 p.m., we headed down to the doctor's office to pick up the test results. After we arrived and had waited in the waiting area for a period of time, we were told to head on back. We went through a door into a long hallway with examination rooms on both sides of the hall. At one point, the doctor stepped out of one of the exam rooms into the hallway. H was holding two manila folders in his hand.

As we approached, he said "Mr. and Mrs. Phillips" and handed us each a folder with our name on it. He said, "You have a clean drug screen. I can assure you that you have not been in a meth lab, or this screen would have picked it up."

I asked him if he would be willing testify as to the validity of the results if it came down to it. I told him why we wanted the test the first time I had met him when he had taken our blood. He told me, "I'll certainly stand behind these tests. I would be glad to testify if it comes to that." I felt like I had just obtained a nice, valuable insurance policy. It felt good. I had real evidence we had not been in a meth lab. The week was turning out pretty good, but it still had one more surprise.

Thursday night, July 31, I received a telephone call from my brother, Paul. He told me a rather strange story. He had received a telephone call from one of our old football players. His name was Mick Stephens. Mick had played linebacker and offensive guard for us back in the early eighties. He had also been our place kicker. He had gone on to become a Shelby County deputy. We had seen him occasionally over the last fourteen years and heard about him and his career from old teammates of his. We had learned that Mick had become a DEA agent.

He told Paul on the phone, "Coach Paul, this is Mick." After the normal phone greetings were exchanged, he added, "Look, I'm calling about Coach Jack. It was my DEA group that was called to his house to investigate the fire in the barn. I was working another case, or I would have been there. I wanted to tell you, Coach, that they know Coach Jack had nothing to do with it, but I'm going to give you the name of a great attorney just in case Coach Jack needs one. This attorney helped me in a couple of excessive force charges as a county deputy. He recently helped me and some other agents when we got busted by a federal game warden for hunting in a baited dove field. He's really good. He has won every case for me. Truthfully, I was guilty every time too. Just tell Coach Jack to call him. I've already told the attorney Coach Jack would be calling. He can probably retain him for ten dollars or so."

Paul thanked Mick for calling. Mick had also told him he was calling from a pay phone and didn't want anyone to know he had called. Paul assured him it would be a guarded secret. So Paul called me and gave me the attorney's name, location, and phone number. He told me he had called the lawyer and set up an appointment for me on Friday, August 1, at 1:30 p.m.

The attorney's name was Lester Moore. He wasn't particularly impressive when I met him, but I did learn he was the retained lawyer for the police association. That meant he was on a really nice retainer. He did have law offices in several different locations around the city. I figured his retainer with the police association was probably at least a half a million dollars a year. Memphis State University had also just fired a popular, favorite-son coach. Mr. Moore was the coach's attorney, and they were negotiating with the university for a buy out of the contract. The coach was in his office when I arrived for my appointment.

I learned in Saturday's paper that the amount of the discussed buy out was 2.5 million dollars. I knew the coach could afford to get the best attorney in town. Besides, I loved and totally trusted Mick. I felt like it was a good move to retain the attorney and have him on our side if we needed him.

When I entered Lester's office, we shook hands, and he told me to take a seat. He said he had talked to Mick and knew the situation.

He said to me, "Look, I want to know one thing: are you guilty or not guilty? Before you answer, give me the ten-dollar retainer fee." I did that. He then continued, "Now, look, I don't really care if you are guilty or not. I will defend you just as vigorously either way. I just don't want to be blindsided by anything. So what is it: guilty or not guilty?"

I told him, "We absolutely haven't done anything illegal. We are not guilty. We had been gone that entire weekend and came back two days early, or we wouldn't have even been there."

He raised his hand as if to stop me and said, "That's good enough. If you need me, Mr. Phillips, I will be your attorney. You have officially retained me. My secretary will give you a receipt for the ten dollars."

He handed me his business card. It had the addresses of his two or three law offices, all the phone numbers, a fax number, and a handwritten cell phone number where I could reach him anytime.

We shook hands, and I left. All in all, it had not been a bad week. I had the clean drug reports for Kara and me, I had retained an excellent lawyer, the burned-out barn had been cleaned up, and Mick, my ex–football player turned DEA agent had said they knew we didn't have anything to do with the meth lab.

It seemed the teachers at school at the in-service meetings had kind of shied away from me, but I passed that off as my own paranoia. Classes would start Monday. I would start weight training with the boys' and girls' track teams and, hopefully, things would return to normal. Thank God! It had been a long stressful time. From the new grandbaby, the car trouble, all the trips, the fire in the barn, having my home searched and being handcuffed. There were certainly a lot of firsts. My hope was these firsts would turn out to also be lasts.

CHAPTER 11

THE NORMALITY
OF WORKING

The second week of August school started, and I met with my track athletes. One hundred ten young men and women showed up to be part of my track program. I set up the week of August 25 for testing to kick off the weight training cycle. After the testing, I set up individualized weight programs for each of the athletes. During the eighth week, we would test again to measure progress and reestablish their individual programs and goals. We utilized "explosive" lifts in this program and some other activities on the off days.

I also found out I had *not* won the teacher of the year competition from the year before. I had certainly tried. After being nominated by my students and chosen as one of the top-five finalists, I had filled out page after page of papers concerning my education philosophy and other questions I had been asked. I felt honored to be one of the five finalists out of twenty-four thousand teachers in Memphis and Shelby County. I wasn't disappointed to not win. I knew winning was a long shot. But as I am a competitive person, it would have been nice to have my teaching ability acknowledged.

About the only problem Kara and I had that fall was juggling the use of the car. I normally went to work around 6:00 a.m. or even earlier. School started at 7:10 a.m. and was dismissed at 2:10 p.m., but the track workouts, practices, and weight lifting usually lasted until at least 4:00 p.m. It was almost a thirty-minute drive from our house to the school. My day normally ran from about 5:30 a.m. until after 4:00 p.m.

On days Kara wasn't working, we didn't have a problem. On days she did work, she needed the car. Her workdays lasted from about 11:00 a.m. or 12:00 p.m. until about 4:00 p.m. or 5:00 p.m. We decided on days she worked, she would get up and take me to school and pick me up when she got off work, around 5:00 p.m. We would get home about thirty minutes later. She often worked Saturdays or Sundays or even an evening shift occasionally. This situation worked itself out pretty well that fall.

August rolled into September. We were back in a familiar routine. On Labor Day, we had friends over for a cookout. It was nice to be around people again. We were still being avoided, or so it seemed to us. By mid-August, a month had passed, and we had not heard a word from any legal authority regarding the fire. We began to breathe a little easier. I think the routine of being back at work had much to do with that feeling.

We had tried to call Donna to see how she was holding up, but her home phone had been disconnected. Her cell phone did not respond to our calls either. She had told us how much she hated Sam Nance and thought he was a bad influence on Timmy. Sam thought he was a ladies' man and always had some younger girl with him. Donna had confided to Kara that she thought Timmy was cheating on her when he left with Sam Nance. In fact, back in March of 1997, she had packed her bags and loaded her car, called us (we had only met her one time at that point), and asked to come hide out at our house. She said she was leaving Timmy.

She had done just that and come to stay with us a few days. I had counseled with her about marriage and urged her to call Timmy and try to get him to come to Memphis to meet with her and talk things over. I told her I would work with them both and try to help them patch up their marriage. Once, while slightly drunk, Sam Nance had actually told me Timmy was having an affair with Donna's sister. I think he said Donna's sister was married to a law enforcement officer and they lived right across the road from Donna and Timmy. Timmy did come down, and he checked into a nearby motel. They never stayed at my house together all night, but they did come over almost each afternoon and evening that March and talked over their marital differences with me. To the best of my knowledge, they are still married. Obviously, Donna never found out about the other woman and that the other woman was her sister (if what Sam Nance had told me was true).

My teaching reached a new high. I had finally arrived and became an effective classroom teacher. Students were transferring (or trying to) to get into my class. I set aside Fridays as special days. We began covering character material from a small book I had. We went through the book line by line and word for word each Friday. Much to my surprise, the students were never late on Friday, never absent, never slept in class, and never caused me any discipline problems on Friday. They saw that I really did care. And I really did! The material we covered on those Fridays proved to be far more important that the routine material we covered in the school curriculum.

However, things were still not quite right. I still had that shadow hanging over me that I could not shake. When it was quiet as the students were taking a test or working on an assignment in class or I was grading papers, I would hear the metal door slam shut the floor below and the echo of footsteps coming up the concrete stairway that opened up right by my classroom door, and I would get a of rush of cold fear. I found myself expecting Agent March to walk through the classroom door.

Was that just fear or a premonition? It was that same old feeling I had when I saw all those plain-clothed men getting out of those vehicles the day of the fire. I felt a great sense of relief when a student or teacher walked through the door instead of Agent March. I would be ashamed of the fear I felt. I thanked God that Agent March never materialized in that doorway. My fears proved to be unfounded.

In late September, we did receive a call from Donna. In fact, she was at one of the hospitals in Memphis. Timmy Tisdale Sr. (Timmy's dad) was in the hospital, dying with cancer. He did eventually die in that hospital. Donna told us she was living at her mother's house in Braggadocio, Missouri. She gave us her new cell phone and home phone numbers. She told us all the charges Timmy was facing in Southeast Missouri for cooking meth. She told us they had multiple dates that the cooks were supposed to have occurred on. However, she didn't believe Timmy was with Sam Nance on every single date. She had an unusual request. She asked if we would be willing to check those dates with our long-distance phone call bills. Often, she and Timmy went to Tunica to the casinos in order for her to keep Timmy away from Sam Nance. She said they often got freebies in the mail for meals and rooms. She did call us many times to try to get us to come down and stay with them. We never did. Often when she called, we weren't home, so she left a number for us to call her back. We had called those numbers in Mississippi several times.

She said she had the discovery evidence from Timmy's case, and it had all the dates. The discovery was back in Missouri at her mom's house. She said she would like to meet with us as soon as possible after she got back to give us a copy with the dates so we could check our long-distance phone bills.

We agreed to meet her and actually did the first Friday night in October. We met at the lounge in the Holiday Inn in Blytheville, Arkansas. She had a copy for us of the discovery from Timmy's case in Missouri. It was about two and a half to three inches thick (a couple of hundred pages). She asked us to take it home and check the dates with our phone bills. Donna cried most of the time we were there. She was so upset. We felt very sorry for her. We offered to let her come stay with us to get away from it all. I told her I could find her a job if she wanted, or she could just stay at our house as long as she needed. I sat down and wrote Timmy a letter when we got home to encourage him and sent the letter along with a new Bible to the jail in Perryville, Missouri.

I took the discovery home and read through it. It was remarkable reading. I jotted down the dates of the Missouri cooks and other events and checked them with our phone bills. There must have been thirty or more dates in the discovery I had to check. Not one of the dates matched the phone calls we had made to Tunica in response to Donna's calls to our house. The evidence against Timmy was overwhelming. This was a huge meth-cooking operation. They had cooked meth close to two dozen times in multiple counties and locations in Missouri. I counted sixty-six names of people involved in that discovery. These were people who had bought supplies, helped them cook, or bought or sold the dope they made for them. It was a huge, complex operation. Timmy was in real trouble.

I couldn't help but notice how well documented all the evidence was in the discovery. I finally found out how the government had obtained such extensive information about this criminal enterprise. The DEA had infiltrated this group in the spring of 1996 (over a year before the bust). They had an undercover agent, Don Ontario, that had bought supplies with them, cooked meth with them, used meth with them, bought meth from them, and was fully embedded in the operation. There were also six other confidential informants (called CIs) in this group feeding law enforcement agencies the information. I wondered why they hadn't busted them months before.

It was a well-coordinated infiltration of a major drug-manufacturing/distribution ring in Southeast Missouri. It was amazing how they had obtained the supplies for this extensive operation. They often loaded up two or three cars with six or more people in a car or van and made supply buying forays up the middle of Missouri, across to St. Louis, over into Illinois, south down through Kentucky, then into Western Tennessee, across the Mississippi River from Dyersburg, Tennessee, to Caruthersville, Missouri, and home again. They stopped all along the way and bought pills by the tens of thousands and ether by the case from farm equipment stores. Even if there had been a few dates I could have helped Donna with, it was obvious Timmy was going to jail.

I particularly scoured the documents, looking for anything that might have been related to the fire at the old barn in Memphis. I was relieved to find not a single mention. Maybe the two weren't involved in that. If they had been, wouldn't it be documented here? Wouldn't the DEA undercover agent at least know about it? Wouldn't one of the CIs have reported it?

Near the end of the discovery, they asked Don Ontario, the DEA undercover agent, if he had ever heard of Jack Phillips or Kara Phillips. They asked him if he knew of any meth cooking with either of them.

He responded, "I've never heard of either one of them." They asked him if he had ever heard of any meth cooking operation in Tennessee. He said, "Sam Nance had once bragged that he had cooked meth in a barn on some professor's property in Tennessee. That is all I have ever heard about anyone cooking meth anywhere in Tennessee."

I showed the statement to Kara. We looked at each other. It was obvious. Sam Nance was responsible for the fire in the barn. We didn't have to say it. That last statement had said everything that could be said.

We had been told the culprits left the fire on motorcycles. Sam Nance had a motorcycle. We had been told eyewitnesses saw two people flee from the fire on motorcycles. We wondered about our friend Timmy. I still discounted the idea because I saw Timmy just five days before the fire. He had a horrible hole through his thigh from the motorcycle wreck and subsequent injury. Also, he had wrecked that motorcycle and had not purchased the new one until after the fire. The black motorcycle I saw at his house was brand-new and didn't have enough miles on it to have been to Tennessee and back (even if he was physically able to make such a trip). Also, would Donna have given me the discovery with that information in it if Timmy had played any part in the fire? No, I didn't think so.

As I neared the end of the discovery papers, I noticed on the last page there was a warning. It cited some law, and it said these papers were part of an ongoing investigation. It said anyone not authorized to have those papers could be subject to a fine and up to ten years in prison if found to have these papers in their possession.

I reasoned that surely couldn't apply here. After all, I had gotten the papers from one of the defendant's spouses. She had asked me to look over the papers and check some dates with my phone records. I called Donna on her cell phone and gave her the bad news that I could not help with any of the dates. I told her about the warning on the last page. She said, "Oh, yeah, you probably need to destroy those papers." We disconnected after she thanked me for trying and told me to say hello to Kara. I grabbed the lighter fluid can and the papers. I went to the trash barrel behind the house, threw the papers in the barrel, doused them with lighter fluid, and set them on fire. I watched as all the pages turned to ash.

CHAPTER 12

A POSTCARD, HOME FOR THANKSGIVING, AND A PHONE CALL

The first week of November, we received a card from Timmy in the county jail. I say *we* because the card was addressed to Mr. and Mrs. Phillips. On the front of the card it said, "In a World of Ordinary People." The message was completed on the inside of the card, where it read, "I Am Glad There Is You".

The sentiment in the message was very moving. Timmy Tisdale was just a country boy in the truest sense of the word. In the seven or eight times I had been around him, I had come away with the idea that he was very guarded with his emotions and feelings. He was just a quiet person. I knew he trained bird dogs for hunting. I could imagine that he was the type that went out into the countryside to train a dog and was more comfortable with the dog than he ever would be socializing with most people.

Even more amazing were the words Timmy had handwritten on the inside of the card.

On the left side, he had said the following:

> Thank you both so much for the Bible. I have
> been reading it. I found out not only would it

not hurt me, but it actually can help me. In fact, it even seems good. I want to thank you both for offering to take care of Donna. I know I am in trouble. It looks like I'll be going to jail. I want to

On the right side of the card, around the message "I'm glad there is you," he wrote the following:

thank you for helping out when we were having problems. You are both real good people and real good friends. Pray for me and Donna and thanks.

Timmy Tisdale

PS: Be sure and ask Donna about the lies Sam Nance plans to tell. It will make you laugh.

We were both left teary eyed after reading the card. We truly felt sorry for Timmy and Donna. Donna had a thirteen-year-old daughter by a previous marriage. She had just started accepting Timmy as a surrogate father. Now it looked like he would be going away for a while.

We called Donna a few days before we were to go home for Thanksgiving and told her about the card and how much we appreciated it. We again offered her a room and support in our home. She said she would think about it. Of course, she cried and thanked us profusely. She asked if we could stop by her mom's when we came home. She assured us it was just a few miles out of the way and right off Interstate 55. We said "Sure," and besides, we wanted to ask her about Timmy's PS in the card. She gave us directions, and we went by there a few days later.

When we arrived at Donna's mother's house, we were introduced to her family and received like we were part of the family. These were good people. She told them about the Bible we had sent Timmy and that he had sent us a warm thank-you card in return.

I told Donna, "The card is in my briefcase in the car. Let me get it and show it to you. You can read it for yourself. Also, you can see read what Timmy told me to ask you about."

As I was getting up to cross the living room, the phone rang. Donna answered it, and we heard her side of the conversation.

"Hello."

"Hi, honey, how are you?"

"Good. I'm fine too."

"Guess who's here, Timmy."

"Jack and Kara."

"Okay."

She said to me, "Jack, would you like to talk to Timmy?"

"Of course," I replied. I grabbed the phone, and we exchanged pleasantries. I asked how he was and if he needed anything. He told me he had everything and thanked me again for the Bible.

I thanked him for the card and said, "That's one reason we are here at Donna's mom's house. I want to ask her about the PS and the lies Sam Nance plans on telling."

There was an extended pause on the other end of the line. Then Timmy said, "Listen, I'll tell you myself, Jack. Jack, it was me and Sam that was cooking meth in the barn and caught it on fire. We caught it on fire and ran."

I interrupted him there and said, "Why haven't you told me? Why didn't you have Donna tell me? Why didn't you tell me when I came to your house after the fire? You just let me rant and rave and tell you all about it when you knew about it all along!"

He said, "Jack, I am sorry. I am sorry for all of it."

I said, "Well, what lies are Sam planning on telling?"

He said, "Sam came to me and told me the DEA knew about the fire in Memphis. I'm going to tell them it was Jack and Phil Richburg that were cooking meth and caught the barn on fire."

I interrupted Timmy again and told him, "I've never met Phil Richburg. I wouldn't know Phil Richburg if he walked up to me right here."

Timmy said, "I know. Now listen, I told Sam I had already told the DEA it was me and him cooking the meth. Nance's exact words were 'You stupid fuck! I ought to kill you!'"

Timmy said Sam grabbed him around the neck with both hands and started choking him. Sam was a pretty big man, and he threw

Timmy to the ground and tried to choke him to death. Timmy said he thought he was going to die.

However, a guard at the jail saw the incident and ran in and pulled Sam off Timmy. Timmy told me Sam was transferred hundreds of miles away to a county jail in Wentzville, Missouri, just west of St. Louis.

I was shocked. I was stunned. I was shocked and stunned! Timmy said, "Jack, you and Kara don't have to worry. I told the DEA you two had nothing to do with it and didn't know nothin' about it."

I sat there for a moment in silence. I said, "Take care of yourself, Timmy. Here is Donna."

I handed the phone back to Donna and went out to the car to get the briefcase with the card. It wasn't that important anymore. I knew Donna and her family wanted to see it. Actually, I wanted a few minutes alone. I climbed in the Camaro and sat behind the wheel. I sat there for a little while, just letting everything sink in.

I ran through my mind all the fear, anxiety, humiliation, intimidation, and oppression that we had gone through since July 13. For four months, it had hung over our heads like a guillotine. I would sort my feelings out later about Timmy and Sam. Now it just felt like a giant load had been lifted off my shoulders. I couldn't wait to tell Kara. I would grab the briefcase, show Donna and her family the card, say my polite good-byes, and get out of that house as fast as I could. I wanted to tell Kara and my mom and dad and brother and kids the news. Although it was cold outside, it felt like warm sunshine had rushed back into our life that cold November day.

We had a great, joyful Thanksgiving with our families and friends. The rest of November was uneventful. We got a lot of our Christmas shopping done early. All the decorations went up. Only Ricky was still living at the house. Even he had kind of stayed away after the fire (I don't know where he stayed). When he heard what Timmy had told me, he began to stay at our house regularly again.

I was notified before the first semester ended that I had again been nominated for teacher of the year. The first semester ended, and all my students passed. The track teams had grown stronger and faster during the off season. I would be moving into a brand-new classroom in a brand-new building in January. I was looking forward to it. I would also find out in January if I was a finalist for the teacher of the year award.

It seemed as if the tide had turned. We had a great Christmas with our families and got to see many old friends. We spent some quality time socializing and relaxing with people we love—both family and friends. It seemed as if the storm had passed.

We returned to Memphis and celebrated New Year's at home, just the two of us. We were still standing. We were optimistic and looking forward to a great 1998.

CHAPTER 13

MORE CLOUDS AND A PRESIDENT'S DAY WEEKEND TO REMEMBER

I chose the first classroom on the right, inside the south entrance to the new building at the school. It was a brand-new two-story large building with twenty-four fully equipped, modern classrooms. There were twelve rooms downstairs and twelve rooms upstairs. I picked the first one on the right downstairs because it had an outside door as well as a door that opened into the hallway. There was a parking place for one car right outside the door of that classroom. It was perfect. I got moved in over the holidays, and the second semester started.

January 1998 had some really nice days. Temperatures rose into the high fifties and low sixties. When it got that warm, our track team went outside and worked out on our days off from weight training. The weight lifting continued. We had time to finish one more cycle, then we would lift only on our in-season maintenance program. The test results were impressive. We had really made some big improvements physically that fall and early winter. Our athletes began to look like athletes. In our few workouts in January, it was obvious we were much better than the year before. I had really only lost about three valuable members from the boys' team and two valuable members from the girls' team through graduation. It was a more mature, experienced, and athletic group of young people. The weight lifting had physically transformed them.

The second week of January, I received notification that I was, indeed, one of the five finalists (again) for teacher of the year. I was the only repeat of the finalists. I spent about two weeks filling out all the forms and answering all the questions associated with the award. I confidently mailed in the papers. I was absolutely convinced I was going to win the award that year. I also felt I deserved the award. I had a double major (history and social studies) and had taught everything from geography to American government. I also had a master's degree from Memphis State University in secondary education and administration. I assumed I would one day be a principal or superintendent.

As a result of my training and later becoming one of only a handful of certified master teachers in all of Tennessee, I was familiar with the tools administrators used to evaluate classroom teachers. I knew how to teach. I had gone through an extensive program to be a master teacher. All my local evaluations were excellent. More importantly, all my students were learning and succeeding. I was a proud schoolteacher.

Kara continued to work part-time at Walmart. Ricky Short was still living at our house, and others came and stayed at our home for various lengths of time. Everyone who came and stayed left our home better than they were when they arrived. We were making a difference in people's lives. We had a bright future and a retirement awaiting us.

Kara's birthday would be on February 19. It would be her forty-fifth birthday. Our cousin, along with her husband, owned several motels, including a few top-end Holiday Inns. One of those was in St. Louis, Missouri. Kara's only living sister was a bartender in the lounge at the fancy Holiday Inn there. Kara's oldest sister had died in a car accident shortly after we had been married. It was a great motel with a large Jacuzzi, indoor pool, and all the amenities. Besides, we could stay there and enjoy it all for free. I called my cousin and made reservations for the weekend of February 20–23 (Friday–Sunday). We knew we could always find something to do in St. Louis. Besides, we would get to visit with Mandy, hear some good country music in the lounge, enjoy the amenities of the hotel, and eat at Rich and Charley's Italian Restaurant.

Thursday, February 12, 1998, would be a date we would never forget. Kara drove me to school that day because she had to work from 11:00 a.m. until 4:00 p.m. I had track practice that day after school, so she would pick me up when she got off work. It was a really nice day. The temperature was in the midsixties. It was the first full day of workouts outside. From now on, we would be outside training hard regardless of the weather. Our first track meet was about six weeks away.

After we finished, I walked around in front of the school and sat down under a tree. I was right by the driveway Kara would use when she came to get me. She showed up at about four twenty-five, and we made the twenty-or-so-minute drive home without incident.

When we got home, we went into the house, and Kara said, "I'm going to the bathroom," and she hurried off down the hall.

I unbuttoned my shirt and took it off, slipped out of my shoes, and began emptying my pockets, putting all the stuff on the television. I couldn't wait to sip into my sweatpants, grab a glass of Mountain Dew, and sat down and rest. It had been a long day.

As I was emptying my pockets, there was a knock at the door just a few feet from where I was standing. It was about 4:55 p.m. I opened the door and got a huge surprise.

No less than eight men with guns drawn burst through the door. They seemed to all be screaming at once. A .45 caliber automatic pistol was stuck in the middle of my forehead. I immediately thought, *Home invasion.* The lead man grabbed me behind the neck and forcibly pushed me back into the den. The others were screaming. I heard one ask, "Where's your wife?"

I told him, "She's in the bathroom."

I was thrown to the floor facedown on the carpet. A knee was placed in my back, my hands and arms were pulled behind my back, and I was handcuffed for the second time in my life. Both times it occurred in the den of my own home. The entire takedown hadn't taken more than ten seconds. I was terrified.

I was even more terrified when I heard our bathroom door being kicked in. I thought about Kara and how much this would scare her. I heard them yell at Kara to get up and pull up her pants. I guess she was on the commode. I turned my head so I could see the entrance to the hallway. I had been extremely terrified. Now I was just getting mad!

There stood my wife, the wife of my childhood, the love of my life, the mother of my children, my best friend, my partner. Tears were running down her face. She was literally sobbing. I mean, weeping harder than I had ever seen her cry. The look on her face, I'll never forget it.

I tried to come up off the floor, but the man with the knee in my back kept me down. He cocked the pistol and pushed it against the back of my skull and said, "Don't move, motherfucker!" No one had ever talked to me like that. No one had ever said anything to me in those words or in that tone of voice. My wife was in full meltdown mode. I had had a gun stuck to my forehead and to the back of my head. My wife and I were now both handcuffed. I had just been called a motherfucker, and we hadn't done anything to anyone.

Wasn't this just another nightmare? This really wasn't happening, was it? Our indignities were not over. I was pulled to my feet, and they read our rights to Kara and me. Miranda warnings. It wasn't a nightmare. This was real. We were officially under arrest! My students and track team members flashed through my mind. My mom and dad too. My brother and his wife, my children, and my grandchildren. I knew that all that had been our life was over just like that.

I couldn't even hear what they were saying to us. I had left that room. My mind was racing—my family! I had never felt so ashamed. Shame! Embarrassed! Ashamed! Angry! Mad! I had never been so mad. I didn't know why I felt so ashamed. It was really strange. I was ashamed and I was being arrested, but I didn't know what to feel ashamed of beyond that.

They led us outside, and there were two vehicles. Both looked like Broncos or Blazers or Pathfinders. One officer grabbed me by the upper arm and led me down the stairs to the passenger side of the first vehicle. Another man had Kara by the upper arm and led her down the stairs and brought her over right next to me.

I hadn't paid much attention to the arresting officers, but the one on the other side of the vehicle was Agent March. His partner is the one who had Kara by the arm. A third agent I hadn't seen before had me by the arm. Four other agents were heading over to the other vehicle. An additional agent was standing behind me, just over my right shoulder. I turned my head and looked at him and couldn't really believe my eyes.

The agent was Mick Stephens, my old football player. He was the person who had called my brother, Paul, and told me to retain Lester Moore as my attorney. I had watched them empty Kara's purse on the coffee table in the living room and just throw her purse on the couch. My billfold and car keys were just laying on the television. It flashed through my mind that I would get one phone call. I thought that was a strange thing for me to be thinking right then. Should I call my brother or my attorney, Lester Moore?

I said to Mick, "Hey, Mick."

He said, "Hi, coach."

I said, "Mick, don't let them do this. You know we would never do this. You know because you have known us over twenty years. You've been to my house many, many times and even eaten at my table. You said at the athletic banquet your senior year that I was more like your dad than your own dad. Don't let them do this. It is wrong. Look at Kara. You know this is wrong!"

Tears were rolling down Mick's face. He was red-faced, but he could not speak. He couldn't look at me either. It was so strange. I was so mad at Mick and the entire situation, but I still loved him and I felt sorry for him. There was no doubt about that.

Agent March, obviously the leader of this mob, shouted across the roof of the Bronco, "Shut the fuck up, or I'll come over there and kick your fuckin' ass!"

I looked at Mick and said, "You're going to let him talk to me like that, Mick? To me? Are you? Why don't you say something? Are you going to let him talk to *me* like that?"

March hollered even louder, "Shut the fuck up, motherfucker, or I'll kick your fuckin' ass!"

I looked at March and said, "I won't shut up. Come on over here and take these handcuffs off and then try to kick my ass!" I looked at Mick and said, "It is time to choose sides, Mick. Take these handcuffs off. Give me a chance. The only way he can whip my ass is if I'm handcuffed."

Mick never uttered a word. He just stood there. The back door was opened, and Kara was shoved into the backseat and then me. March got in on the driver's side, and his partner got in on the passenger side. I never saw Mick Stephens again.

For the next thirty-five minutes or so, we were taunted, verbally abused, and cursed by the two thugs in the vehicle disguised as Federal Drug Enforcement agents. They were a disgrace to their badges. We had not even been convicted of any crime but were being treated as criminals by these two, who wanted to be judge and jury and executioner as well. They continually looked in the rearview mirror at me in the backseat and said things like the following:

"How you feel now, Mr. Teacher and Coach?"

"How does it feel to know your wife is going to prison?"

"You're going to be man enough to do the time, Phillips?"

Whey they had been at the house back in July, I had overheard March talking about his son playing baseball on the Dodgers, one of the youth traveling baseball teams. He was playing somewhere that Sunday afternoon of the fire. I couldn't resist telling him, "March, you know you've got two innocent people, and you are doing this anyway. Whatever you do to us will come back on your son and any other children you might ever have. All of this will come back on you."

He stomped on the brakes of the truck and pulled over on the side of the four-lane highway bypass. He turned around, reached across the backseat, and pointed his gun right between my eyes, only inches from my face. He came unglued. I discovered he was good at dishing it out, but he couldn't take it. He said, "One more word, you son of a bitch, and I'll blow your fucking brains all over this truck. Shut the fuck up!"

Kara told me to not say anything else. I am sure she believed he would do just as he said he would. I can't say if I thought he would or wouldn't. I can say it didn't seem to matter to me one way or another at that moment. I really didn't care. I was calm and composed just as I had been as a player and as a coach with the game on the line and all the pressure on me. As others went crazy around me, I calmed down.

I looked him in the eye and said, "You won't do anything to me. You're all talk. You're more of a criminal that either one of us. You shoot me, and your career is over. Your life is over. Your son won't ever see his daddy again, so turn around and drive."

His partner grabbed him and said, "It's not worth it, Mike."

We drove on. We arrived downtown at what is known in Memphis as 201 Poplar. It had gotten dark by the time we pulled into the underground garage to park. We went upstairs into the building and down a hallway. One agent led Kara away in one direction, and they took me in another direction. I was placed in what was called a holding cell with about fifteen other men.

They had let me put my shirt and shoes and coat on at the house before we left. I had on the same clothes I had worn to school at around 5:30 a.m. on that Thursday morning, February 12, 1998.

INTO THE BELLY
OF THE BEAST

The holding cell was about sixteen feet by eight feet. Opposite the door was a metal commode and sink combo (no lid on the commode). They were built into the wall. Two benches were attached to the walls, one bench on each side of the cell.

There were fifteen men crowded into the cell. One man had to stand up because of the crowding. He stood by the sink/commode. As they brought me in, they took another man out, so I grabbed the seat he had vacated on the bench. I took stock of the men in the room with me. They looked rough. God only knows what they had been arrested for. They smelled too—no, they stunk. I could smell them and smell the nasty room too. It smelled like urine and fear and puke. I could smell the body odor. It was way too close in the small cell.

There was a least one identical holding cell next door. I had seen that cell when I had been brought in. Both cells had their doors standing open, I guess, because it was so hot in the cells and smelled so badly. One of the men in my holding cell was telling some of the other men how two weeks before, a body had been found underneath the bench where I was sitting. He had crawled under the bench to go to sleep. It was crowded then too, and there was no place to sit. I looked across the room and noticed, for the first time, that there was a man apparently asleep under the bench on the opposite wall right then. I looked, but there was no one sleeping under my bench. The guy went on with the story and told how the man had stayed under the bench the week before for three days before anyone noticed he was dead. He said that partly accounted for the funky smell in the cell.

As the night went on, officers continued to bring more men in and take more men out. I learned from the conversations that these men were being booked into the jail. That meant mug shots, fingerprints, and emptying your pockets. All your valuables—watches, billfolds, money, etc.—would be placed in a large clasp envelope with your name on it.

Very little conversation was going on. Then a rumble happened next door. Chaos broke loose. I guess an arrestee began physically wrestling with an officer. We all heard the noise, then heard a hiss, and smelled the mace that had been sprayed. The man scuffling with the police was screaming and ranting and then complaining how much it burned! We heard handcuffs rattle and the door slam shut next door. The mace filled up the entire holding area. It crept into our cell, burning our noses and eyes. The men in my cell began complaining loudly, so the authorities just came over and slammed our door shut too.

With our door now closed and locked, everything in our cell became more pronounced. The smell was worse. One large black man got up, sat on the commode, and took a dump right at that moment. All at once, the man that had been standing by the sink just lost it. He began panting and started running full speed right into the door, back and forth, slamming into the door over and over again. He was screaming at the top of his lungs, "Let me out!" I wondered if he was claustrophobic. His rants became unintelligible yet louder. He continued to bang into the door over and over. I had never witnessed such despair (or insanity). It was heartbreaking, mind-numbing, and fascinating to watch. I wondered if I might end up doing the same thing. I knew it was possible. I wondered how Kara was making out wherever she was.

The man was really getting on all our collective nerves in that holding cell. Finally, an old man sitting next to me said, "That's enough, crackhead! Sit down! Sit down! Sit down now! You're driving us all nuts."

Someone got up out of their seat and let the young man sit down. He was exhausted and breathing very heavily. About that time, the door opened, and they gave each of us a sandwich (it was egg, turkey, or chicken salad—I'm not sure which) and a small cup of Kool-Aid. I was starving. I hadn't eaten anything since a hamburger at lunch at school. When I took a bite of the sandwich, I gagged. It was disgusting. I knew I had to eat, so I balled up the sandwich into a tight ball and began taking small bites out of it and chewing and swallowing as quickly as possible. I forced down the sandwich.

About 10:30 p.m., they finally got to me. There weren't but two of us left in the cell by then. I guess the Memphis Police Department wasn't too busy that Thursday night, February 12, 1998. They took my mug shot from about five different angles. Then they took my fingerprints from a messy ink pad (first time I had had a mug shot taken or my fingerprints). I had nothing in my pockets for them to take because all my possessions, including my watch, were lying on the television in my house. They also let me make a phone call. I called Paul. He told me he would call Lester Moore immediately and see about getting my out. I knew it would be the next day at the earliest.

The officers doing the booking didn't seem to know what to do with me. I know now it was because I was federal and not state. Finally, about 1:00 a.m., they took me into a hallway. There were locked office doors down both sides of the hallway and not a human being in sight. I was not even handcuffed. The hallway was probably fifty or sixty feet long. I still had on my dress pants and shoes and shirt that I had worn to work that morning. I still had on my red jacket with the gray hood. That helped. It was cold in the hallway. I had nowhere to sit except on the floor for a few hours. I finally lay over on the cold tiled floor and went to sleep.

I wondered about Kara. The last eight hours had been horrendous for me. I know it was probably worse for her. I was having trouble holding it together. Was she managing to hold it together? Was she losing it like the man in my holding cell? For the first time since I started dating her on August 8, 1967, I could not protect her at all. She was at the mercy of…who knows what!

CHAPTER 15

IN A CELL

They put me in a cell, with bars and all, on a range with about forty other cells. It was about 5:00 a.m. Finally, they put a young boy in the cell with me. He was wearing a sweatshirt and blue jeans. He couldn't have been over twenty-one years of age. All I had was a metal bunk—no covers, pillows, or sheets.

He told me he had violated parole and knew they would be coming for him. He sat down on the floor in the middle of the cell and began unraveling the hem on the pant legs of his blue jeans. In one hem, he had roll-your-own tobacco and rolling papers. In the other hem, he had marijuana and books of paper matches all rolled up. He offered me some, but I declined. He rolled up one of each and lit up and smoked. He hollered and got some answers from the other inmates along the range. He must have known most of them.

Soon, they were passing cigarettes, joints, and matches all up and down the range. They used a piece of string anchored with an empty Bic lighter. They just tied whatever they wanted to pass on the string, shoved it under the door, and threw the lighter from cell to cell. It really was quite ingenious. They brought breakfast, but mine seemed to be crawling on the tray. I couldn't think about eating it. The kid ate every bite of his and all of mine as well. It was more than obvious he had been here before.

At about 8:00 a.m., a guard told me to get ready as I was going to federal court to be arraigned. I knew that meant "officially charged."

They allowed me a phone call about ten minutes later. I called Paul, and he told me Lester Moore, my attorney, would be in court with me. He said Lester had called him and told him I would be arraigned this morning and they would set bond. My brother was going to wait at home until the bond was set, borrow the money, and come bail me out. He just needed to know the exact amount. Lester told him he would call and tell him the amount of money he needed to bring. They did not accept personal checks. Everything seemed to be set.

Two officers showed up about 8:50 a.m. to get me out and escort me to the federal building just across the plaza. It was about a five-minute walk. We were all surprised when the electronic door to my cell would not open. They checked the other doors and found that all the doors on all the cells on the range opened except mine and the one next to mine.

Three men showed up—I realize now they were probably inmate trustees who worked as electricians—to fix the cell doors. They had a ladder that they used to reach a square box that ran the length of the hallway. One of the men climbed up the ladder right across the hall from my cell and removed the end cover of the metal box. When he did, a huge wad of multicolored wires fell out into his hands.

I stood at the door of the cell and watched them work almost directly across the hallway from my cell door. The escort guards came by and told me my arraignment had been moved to 11:00 a.m. I watched the men continue to work on the wires. They stripped them and taped wires together. Then they put the cover back on after they stuffed the wires back in the box and tried to open the doors. No luck. The doors would not open.

They simply opened the box again, pulled the wires out, removed the tape they had used, and then rewired and retaped their work. They did this repeatedly. Each time, they put the cover back on the box, tried the doors, but they would not open.

I began to pay more attention to what they were doing. Finally, I told them, "Hey, why don't you try connecting the wires by color? Put the black wires together, the red wires together, the blue wires together, the green wires together, and so on, and then tape them together." They looked at me, then at each other, and then just shrugged and began matching the wires by color and taping them together. Amazingly, the doors opened. I was escorted to the federal building about 10:55 a.m. It looked like I would make the 11:00 a.m. arraignment.

We had no more than got to the seventh floor and been placed in the holding cell when a US marshal appeared and said, "Relax, Phillips, they've moved your hearing to 1:00 p.m." He told me and the other twelve men in the holding cell they would bring us lunch in a few minutes. The lunch was much, much better than what I would have gotten at 201 Poplar. This food was catered. More importantly, I knew I would be eating my next meal at home as soon as our bond was posted. I was anxious for the hearing because I would get to see Kara there too.

I told one of the men I sure didn't want to go back to 201 Poplar. He told me after I was arraigned I could not go back to 201 Poplar because the jail there didn't meet federal standards and could not house federal inmates. I asked him if that was true for women too. He didn't know.

The men in the holding cells were steadily going in and out of the holding cells. Some were being arraigned like me, some were going for hearings, some were actually on trial, and others were being sentenced. Most of the men in the holding cells had on prison-issued clothes. I was still in my street clothes. I found out most of them were being held at a private prison located in Mason, Tennessee. It was owned by Correction Corporation of America (CCA). That was where they held federal prisoners at this stage.

One o'clock rolled around, then one thirty, and finally, a US marshal came in and said, "Phillips, you'll go in at 3:30 p.m." Kara was already there when I arrived. That was the best thing. I met Lester Moore again and shook hands with him. He told me to be quiet and let him do all the talking for Kara and me.

They read the charges against us and asked how we pled. We pled "Not guilty." I also got my first look at Terry Descussio, the assistant United States attorney. DEA Agent Mike March was with him. It was hard to tell which one of them looked the sleaziest. If a person looked at our table, then at their table, he would have thought they were the defendants, not us.

After the charges were read and entered, they began discussing bond. It was unbelievable to me, but the AUSA was asking for no bond for me and a $5,000,000 bond on Kara! Thank God the magistrate judge just laughed. They put me on the stand to testify about our finances. It came out that we had no passport, didn't even own our car or house, and were actually deeply in debt.

My lawyer was trying to hurry the process along. A court clerk in the courtroom was actually on the phone with my brother, Paul, who was sitting at his house, waiting to hear the amount he needed to bring. She assured my brother on the phone that she would wait for him to arrive with the money once the bond was set. It was 4:50 p.m. The courthouse normally closed at 5:00 p.m. The magistrate finally set our bond. Mine was set at $7,500 and Kara's at $5,000.

It would take $1,250 (10 percent) for us to be released on bond. My brother told the clerk he was on his way, and she reported that to the magistrate. He adjourned the court. My lawyer said he would be up to see us in just a few minutes.

We were both escorted back upstairs (not handcuffed) and placed in small room together. The door was even left standing open. We were told to wait there. We were finally alone together. We cried a little and hugged a lot. We were anxious to get out of there—to get out of custody—and to get back home.

At about 6:00 p.m., we heard rattling metallic sounds and voices outside the room in the hallway around the corner. Two US marshals appeared in our doorway with handcuffs and chains. They told us to step out of the room.

I said, "Wait a minute. Our bond has been set. My brother is bringing the money. The clerk agreed to wait for him. Just call her and ask her."

He said, "Sir, the building has been closed since 5:00 p.m. No one can get in the building. Your brother's not going to post your bond today."

Kara was asking, "Jack, what's going on? They set our bond."

I didn't know. I just knew we were being handcuffed and shackled. We had been handcuffed twice before. We had never been shackled. Kara was crying. It was Friday. The court wouldn't be open on the weekend. It was also President's Day Weekend on Monday, a national holiday. The court wouldn't be open until Tuesday of next week. We were both going to jail.

I had seen people handcuffed and shackled on TV. I had never realized how uncomfortable and demeaning it was. I couldn't walk. I could only shuffle along. I guess that was the whole idea. My god! I looked at Kara and was sick all over.

They took Kara away first in one direction and me in the other direction. I yelled at Kara, "Stay strong. It'll be okay." She didn't reply. I asked where I was going. They told me, "To prison."

CHAPTER 16

FIVE DAYS IN PRISON

found out later from Kara that she had been taken back to 201 Poplar and placed in a cell on a range with other offenders. She said the food was horrible and she didn't eat anything the entire five days. She said she was locked up with all kinds of offenders, including one woman that had killed two of her own children and another who had killed her own husband and eaten his flesh. She said she was scared to death and didn't look at or speak to anyone unless spoken to the entire time she was there.

I was stuck in a van with about ten other shackled men. Most of them, maybe all of them, had been in the holding cells earlier with me at the federal courthouse. Some of them were already being housed at CCA Mason. In fact, I might have been the only new man.

We arrived at the private prison about 8:00 p.m. Most of the men were simply unshackled and returned to the unit where they had already been assigned. I was taken into a small office that had a small holding cell in the back. The holding cell was relatively small. They put me in there and locked the door. It was dirty in there, but not as bad as 201 Poplar. I realized how exhausted I was and eventually fell asleep thinking about how hungry I was.

Eventually, they unlocked the door. An officer handed me a bedroll with sheet, blanket, and a small pillow. He told me to strip off all my clothes. I did so. He handed me a pair of socks, boxer shorts, a T-shirt, a slip-on V-neck maroon-colored shirt and matching pants that had an elastic waist. He added a pair of cheap slip-on blue tennis slippers.

The officer asked me if I wanted to donate my clothes or keep them. I told him I wanted to keep them. He had me place all my clothes (including shoes) into a cardboard box. It was taped, and my name was scribbled across the top of the box.

He told me to grab my bedroll and he would take me to my cell. We went down the hallway a little ways and made a left. There were red lines on each side of the hallway about three feet from the walls. He told me to stay between the red line and the wall.

We went almost all the way to the end of that hallway to the last two doors. These doors were electronically controlled. There was an elevated control room between them staffed by a small female officer. There was a small lobby (sally port) inside each door then another locked door that led into two cell blocks. The cell block on the right was lettered with a large A. The cell block on the left, where I was taken, was labeled B.

The door popped open, and we entered the large dayroom in unit B. It was really large and had a high ceiling. There were ten metal tables scattered across the dayroom; each table had four attached metal stools for seating. There were four or five shower stalls on the right wall next to the door I had just entered. The stalls were separated by small walls about three feet high. There was another three foot wall that ran the length of the shower area with an attached concrete bench facing the showers. There was no privacy at all. The female officer in the control booth (or bubble) was a mere twenty feet away or so. From where she sat, she would be able to literally see it all. So would anyone else in the dayroom.

There were ten cells with doors downstairs and ten cells with doors upstairs. There was about a four-foot-high wall running down the length of the hallway in front of the upstairs doors. There was also a TV mounted on the wall in the dayroom. It was opposite the cells and about twentu feet off the floor. It was on full volume, but the acoustics were so bad I couldn't make out anything being said on the TV. It was midnight, but there were three or four men sitting around tables playing cards, watching TV, or just talking. There was a concrete kiosk in the dayroom with four telephone bays. These were just seats built into the concrete kiosk. However, only three of them actually had telephones. Most of the doors to the cells were closed. There were a few men standing along the wall upstairs outside their cells. All eyes were on me, the new guy.

I guess it was natural that everyone wanted a look at the new man. The guard took me to the stairs on the right side. We went up the stairs and then across the range. We stopped at cell 204. He knocked on the door. The door buzzer sounded, and then the door popped open. A redheaded country boy came to the door in the same clothes I was wearing. I went in and met Byron South. He was called Country. When he opened his mouth to speak, it was easy to see why. He was from Tupelo, Mississippi. Three other men came into the room and introduced themselves. Obviously, these four men were friends, or at least an informal group. They lived in the next two cells down the range, in 206 and 208.

For the next four days, I would get my introduction to life in prison. It was so cold in those cells at night that ice in a cup would not melt. Little cartons of milk would freeze solid if you put it on a windowsill. I would be there until sometime Tuesday. I wrapped myself in a blanket and stayed wrapped up for the next four days. I was cold the entire time. We were allowed to go to Rec one hour in the morning and one hour in the afternoon. Rec was a large fenced-in yard with a dirt track a person could walk around or an old gymnasium.

The five guys I met took care of me that weekend and shared everything they had with me. My brother could send money, but the store didn't open again until Tuesday, so I wouldn't get to shop. I told them to give me their names and numbers and I would have my brother send some money to one of their accounts. A guy named Will Childers gave me his and explained the process of sending money. The other guys all said, "Send it to Will. He doesn't have anyone out there to send him any money." Will was a truck driver by trade. Later, as I was leaving, I told them I would send Will $25 a week as soon as I got out. I don't think they believed me.

I did call my brother, but the fifteen-minute collect call cost $7.50. He sent Will $25. It posted immediately. The other four men seemed surprised that I had actually followed through with what I said I would do. I thought it was the normal and right thing to do.

One of the men had purposely violated his parole and came back to prison for one year. In doing the year, he would fulfill his entire parole obligation. He told me how he did his time. He would stay up until midnight each day then sleep until noon the next day. He slept twelve hours a day. He explained that by dong his time that way, he would only be awake for half the time.

I found out from Paul that Kara was still at 201 Poplar. I felt sorry for her. I was in a much-better place than she was. Time literally crawled by. I was furious we were even in jail. Our bond had been set. My brother had the money. The clerk promised to wait. We should have had our hearing at 9:00 a.m. as scheduled, and none of this would have happened. I realized suddenly that the entire delay had probably been on purpose.

Saturday night, as I was standing near the wall outside my cell upstairs, I was watching the Memphis news on television. I couldn't understand what was being said, but I could see it well enough. I was about eye level with the TV. All of a sudden, my face filled the entire TV screen. My name scrolled along the bottom of the picture. It was just like the image I had seen on the CBS affiliate out of Cape Girardeau, Missouri, that showed Timmy Tisdale's and Sam Nance's faces. Everyone I could see from where I stood in the dayroom, downstairs, and upstairs turned and looked up and pointed at me. They would look at the TV then look back up at me. Now, millions of people would know we had been arrested. Then they showed the front door of my house. The door was open. Everyone could also see my dad's car in front of my house. I knew my car was behind the house.

I rushed down the stairs and waited for a phone. I called my house but got no answer (Ricky Short wasn't there). I called Paul. He had seen the newscast. He said there had been a big story on the front page of the *Commercial Appeal* that morning as well as a photo of me. The story in the paper had given my address. It had said at the time we had not posted bond and were still in jail.

Paul rushed over to the house and found everything was still there. He took all our valuables, locked up the house, took our keys, and arranged to have both automobiles moved to his house. We remained the lead story on the local news on Sunday and Monday as well. This was not going away.

They woke me up at 2:00 a.m. Tuesday morning, and they took me back to the holding cell behind the little office. I changed back into the clothes I had worn over there. I had been arrested in those clothes on Thursday. They were filthy and wrinkled badly. I was glad to get my coat back. Finally, maybe I could get warm. About 8:00 a.m., they shackled me and about six other men going to court in Memphis. I was ready to leave Mason.

I had said my good-byes to my friends there and promised I would send the money to Will. They said okay, but now I know they didn't believe me at all. I have since found out that it is common for those leaving to make similar promises but unheard of for someone to actually do it. I sent $25 every week for the next twenty-four weeks.

I got to the courthouse about 8:55 a.m. I was led straight to the clerk's office. Paul was already there waiting. He had to be restrained when he saw me in shackles. Kara came in right behind me, and they took the shackles off her. We cried a lot and held on to each other for dear life. Paul paid the $1,250 and got the receipt, and we walked out into the sunlight.

We had to go by and see the probation officer, so we walked over to the next building. We listened to his speech and got a list of rules and a map of where we were allowed to travel. We left the office and were finally free again. At least for a while.

WHAT NOW?

We couldn't get away from that federal building fast enough. It had been intimidating to see the following:

UNITED STATES OF AMERICA

v.

JACK AND KARA PHILLIPS

All I could think was the most powerful nation in the history of the world was now against us. Paul took us to his house. That was fine with us. It was a good thirty-minute drive. Memphis never looked so good.

Of course, Paul wanted to know all about what we had been through, but Kara and I were not really in a talkative mood. I guess we were both in some kind of postarrest syndrome. In other words, we were completely in shock. We couldn't wrap our minds around what we had been through and what had just happened to us.

I knew I had two phone calls to make. First, I wanted to call my mom and dad. I felt like I should apologize and explain or either explain then apologize. They received the Memphis news on channel 13 in Rector too. I felt guilty even though technically I had done nothing to bring this about. I wanted my mom and dad to know and hear it from me that I was totally innocent, and at the same time, I wanted them to know I was so sorry I had brought disrepute on the family name. Secondly, I wanted to call Lester Moore to set up a meeting and arrange to pay him his fee for his services. He had never come up to see us as he had promised to do after the arraignment while we were waiting for Paul to bring the bond money.

We arrived at Paul's, and I was able to make both telephone calls. My parents were only concerned about our welfare and not at all about how this might or might not have affected them. Lester Moore set up an appointment with us for Wednesday afternoon at 1:00 p.m. It would be the first time we would be meeting with him since we had been arraigned.

I also called the school and left a recorded message that I would not be at school Wednesday. We settled in at Paul's and spent Tuesday night at his home.

We got up early Wednesday, and after Paul and Jenny left for school (they were both schoolteachers), we jumped in our car and went home. The last time we had been there was Thursday, February 12, 1998, the day we were arrested. Paul had already picked up all our valuables—billfold, credit cards, Kara's purse, our car keys, etc.—and returned them to us. Truthfully, there were a lot of conflicting emotions as we turned into the driveway.

For some reason, I pulled the car behind the house. It felt safer if no one knew we were home, for some reason. We immediately closed up all the blinds and locked all the doors. We both knew it was futile, but if they came to arrest us again, we wanted to delay it for as long as possible. We climbed in the bed and grabbed a few more hours of sleep. It felt good to be in our own home and in our own bed.

We had a sandwich for lunch and then drove to Lester's office. He did the same song and dance about not caring if we were innocent or guilty, but he did want to know the truth. We adamantly claimed our innocence. He told us it would cost ten thousand dollars for him to represent us and that it would cost thousands more if we pled "Not guilty" and actually went to trial. He said normally he would charge us each that amount, but since we were relatively broke, he would only charge us the one fee. I knew Mom and Dad would remortgage their house if we needed the money. I guess the most memorable thing that came out of the meeting was that Lester Moore told us at some point that we could get up to ten years if we went to trial and were found guilty. Ten years was a lot of time. He also told us that Kara had only been arrested in an effort to force me to plead guilty. I asked Lester how much time I would get if I pled guilty. He said he didn't know, but he was sure at some point the AUSA would make us an offer.

He told us he would file a motion for all discovery (evidence) the government had against us and then we would meet again. He told us to begin preparing a notebook with all our witnesses and to write down all that they could testify to on our behalf. He said he would call us for our next appointment and that if anything else came up, to call him immediately.

We told Lester we would probably go to Rector at the end of the week. We gave him the pertinent phone number where we could be reached there. He told us something else we found surprising. He said, "If you go there, don't stop on the interstate for any reason. Even if an officer tries to pull you over, don't stop. Put on your emergency flashing lights, slow down, and drive to the nearest exit with a well-lit public area, like a restaurant or truck stop or quick shop."

I asked, "Why?"

He said, "So they don't pull you over, search your car, and plant something on you."

I couldn't believe it. I told him I didn't think they would plant anything on me or in my car. His response was "Think again!"

We left his office and stopped at a Blockbuster and rented three movies. Then, we went to the grocery store to do some much-needed shopping. We didn't stay there too long. It seemed to us that everyone in the store recognized us and seemed to be talking about us. We grabbed the bare essentials and got out of there. We had discovered we were notorious (or maybe infamous).

We got back home and once again parked the car behind the house. We carried in the movies and the groceries. Kara began preparing supper. I walked down the driveway to the mailbox by the highway out front. It was crammed full of mail, about five days' worth. One of the letters immediately caught my attention. It was from Shelby County Schools. It informed me I had been placed on administrative leave until our legal matter was resolved. I was told *not* to show up at school for work. I was on a twelve-month contract, so I would at least continue to draw my pay until the contract expired at the end of July. Kara called Walmart and told them she was quitting her job. They told her she could pick up her last paycheck anytime after 4:00 p.m. on Friday. Walmart seemed to know our legal situation too. With all the publicity, I guess everyone did.

As Kara finished supper, we settled in to watch a couple of movies. We kept all the lights off so it looked like no one was home from the outside. Ricky Short was still officially living with us. At least, his clothes were still there. It was obvious he was going to stay away.

It was odd that our telephone never rang all day. I knew Paul would call later that night, but not having a phone call all day just didn't happen at our house. If we felt like others believed us to be toxic before, it was obvious we had now gone from toxic to hazardous. No one wanted to be associated with us in any way.

I couldn't help wondering what I would do with my time. I had been going to work early in the morning for over thirty years. Now, for the first time in my adult life, I had no reason to get up in the morning and nowhere to go when I did.

The probation officer had given us a map that showed where we were allowed to travel. It included West Tennessee, Northeast Arkansas, and Southeast Missouri. Any other travel was restricted and would have to be approved on an as-needed basis. If we were leaving the state, we were given a phone number to call to let the probation office know where we were going and when we would be coming back. We were also told to leave phone numbers where we could be reached while out of state.

Thursday morning, we returned the movies and rented three more. Later that morning, our phone rang. It was the probation office calling. We were told to both report to the office of the probation service at 9:00 a.m. Friday. We spent Thursday night still hiding out in our home. We watched movies and went to bed early. It was Kara's forty-fifth birthday. It was the first time we had been intimate since our arrest. We both needed the intimacy. I was reminded to call my cousin and cancel our reservations in St. Louis at the Holiday Inn for the upcoming weekend.

We left the house at about 8:00 a.m. on to go to the probation office. We had packed our bags and decided to just leave from there to go on to Rector for the weekend. When we arrived at the probation office, we were told we both had to give urine samples for drug tests. They told us we would be scheduled for a drug test each month and there would also be random tests given. We weren't worried about the tests, but it took about forty-five minutes to drive there and it cost eight dollars just to park. Also, we dreaded it because we had to go into the federal building to reach the probation office. That building held bad memories for both of us.

We informed the probation officers we were going to Rector for most of a week. We gave them the relative phone numbers, did the test, left, and drove home to Rector, Arkansas.

It was nice to be home with the family. They were all very supportive, but I felt something had changed. We had been inside. No one on either side of our families could relate to what we had been through. Kara and I grew closer.

We stayed a full week. We wanted to be there on the twenty-fourth because it was our eldest grandson's sixth birthday. What we discovered was that we were just as toxic there as we had been in Memphis. We had one, just one, female friend that saw our car and came by our parents' house. All our friends saw our car, but none stopped by. Normally, four of five different friends would have been calling and wanting us to come over to their house for this or that. No one called. No one stopped by except the one female friend. So much for our lifelong friendships. With the exception of the one friend, we were cut off. It hurt us both. It still hurts.

I guess the other thing that really struck us was that we had to travel with a real fear of being stopped and having something planted in our car. It didn't make any sense that anyone on earth would go to that extent to cause us trouble. It bothered both of us. We must have really offended someone somewhere of something.

CHAPTER 18

BIDING OUR TIME

Our trip to Rector and back to Memphis was uneventful. We arrived home the night of the twenty-seventh. We didn't get pulled over. Of course, I made sure to meticulously follow every traffic law. I even walked around the car to make sure all the headlights and taillights were working properly. We had been told to report immediately any and all encounters with law enforcement. We didn't want to do anything to jeopardize our bail and have to sit in jail until the time of our trial.

Kara had commented that she dreaded going home. That was a first for us both. We had both come to love that little house. It had truly been a home for us and a refuge for others. That house had always been filled with love. Now, it seemed cold and uninviting, like it had been violated too. We picked up some more movies and parked the car behind the house. We ordered pizza and settled in for a Friday night at home.

Ricky Short came home that night, and we caught him up on everything that had happened. It was good to have him there. We needed a friend. He volunteered to go to the grocery store for us since we felt so intimidated by everyone's reaction or imagined reaction to us—stares, whispers, etc. Ricky would be a permanent figure at our house for the next four months. He proved he was a real friend.

I also received my first of many calls from Byron Smith, my old cellmate from my five days at CCA Mason. He told me he was being transferred to the federal correctional institute in Memphis. It was a medium-high security facility not ten minutes from our house. He told me what he could about Will and the other men from CCA. He told me they were all surprised that I had actually sent money as I said I would.

Of course, I was in continual contact with Paul. He and Jenny dropped by on Saturday for a few hours. We wanted to go to church on Sunday, but we realized two accused individuals like us would not likely be welcome in any church we knew. We were hurting. We both found it sad that we as Christians had nowhere to go to church. I think it made a big statement about the condition of our churches in Memphis and this country.

Neither of us was sad to see February roll over into March. February had been a total disaster. We hoped March would be an improvement. I should add that Kara and I valued every day we had free and together. The five-day separation over President's Day weekend had been a wake-up call. We would no longer take each other for granted. There was a renewed love and passion between us. After twenty-seven years of marriage, we were like high school kids again with each other. We couldn't keep our hands off each other and couldn't bear to be out of each other's sight for very long.

Even as our so-called friends withdrew and separated from us, we grew closer and held on to each other for dear life. We began to place an extremely high value on our love, our marriage, and our friendship with each other.

CHAPTER 19

LEGAL TIMES

Kara and I worked hard on two particular things related to our case. First, we fixed up calendars that traced each of our activities from the end of school in May 1997 through July 13, 1997. We discovered that Kara had only been home six nights that summer and I had only been home thirteen nights. We had been gone almost all summer. With the help of our Exxon travel card receipts, motel receipts, and Mary Lynn's trips in and out of the hospital with false labor pains, we had put together quite an extensive travel log.

Secondly, we began filling out our book of witnesses and what they could testify about. In only a few days, we had twenty-seven names in our book and over fifty pages of notes detailing the testimony each witness could give. There were other people, like Donna Tisdale, that we would have included in our witness list, but we knew we really couldn't use her. The witnesses ranged from our children and other family members to students, athletes, people that had lived in our home, and even our pastor that had married us in 1970.

Dr. John Henson, my pastor, and I had a conversation at the school in the teacher's lounge in the middle of March 1997. I had not seen Brother John (as we had called him) for over twenty-five years. I had a planning period right before lunch. When I walked into the teacher's lounge, I was surprised to see Brother John sitting at a table there. He was the only other person in the room. He was substituting for a teacher at my school that day.

It was a nice reunion. I discovered he lived right around the corner from me. He passed by my house multiple times each day. I caught him up on everything that had been going on in our lives. I told him how I had started dealing with adults and their problems. I related how many people had lived at our house over the preceding year and what kind of problems many of them had. He was not only a pastor with a doctorate in theology but he was also a Christian counselor. He was one person who could relate to what Kara and I were doing with our lives. After listening, he said to me, "Jack, I'm not telling you to stop what you are doing. It is obvious God has opened a door of ministry for you to do. However, I do want to warn you about one thing. When you let people come to live at your home, remember, their problems have a way of becoming your problems. They tend to leave their problems at your doorstep. As I said, I'm not trying to tell you this so you'll stop what you are doing. I am just giving you fair warning."

It was the next Sunday night in March 1997 that Savanna Nance showed up at our house. Her presence in our home proved to be the foot in the door that would end up allowing Sam Nance and Timmy Tisdale to discover the old barn on the property and end up cooking meth there and catching the barn on fire. Brother John's warning proved to be prophetic.

We had not only prepared the calendars and the witness book but we had also put together telephone records, school purchase orders requests, and everything we could find related to our activities from May 1997 through July 13, 1997. We added our lease that showed clearly that we only rented/leased a house on the property at 711 Highway 72 and not a barn. It showed we had no legal connection to the barn where the fire had occurred. We took photos of the For Sale sign in our front yard that said the property had been zoned Commercial and listed the real estate company and a phone number to call. Lastly, we added the drug tests we had taken seven months earlier, the teacher of the year nominations I had received over the last two years, and a year's worth of bank statements. It was quite a collection of evidence that we had managed to compile.

It seemed obvious (at least to us) that if any reasonable person looked at our documentation, it would be clear we were not involved in drugs in any way. Nothing in our history—past, present, or future—indicated any involvement with drugs. The drug tests showed we had not been in any lab cooking any drugs or taking drugs, and the bank account showed we had not profited from drugs. I couldn't wait to get everything to Lester Moore, our attorney.

The probation office called and told us to report March 17 for our monthly drug tests. They also warned us that my probation officer and Kara's probation officer would be dropping by unannounced at our home for random checks on us. We told them we were parking our car behind the house so even if it looked as if we were not there, we probably were there.

Lester Moore's office finally called and set up an appointment for us the next Thursday in March, but it got canceled. We were called back to court on March 30, 1998. At that hearing, our attorney, Lester Moore, asked for a continuance. We had a new report date of April 13, and the trial was scheduled for May 4, 1998.

It was at this March hearing that the presiding magistrate judge, Richard Hunt, ordered that Kara and I have separate counsel. He said the purpose was to avoid a possible conflict of interest. We argued about it, but we lost the argument. That meant Lester Moore could represent one of us and the other would have a court-appointed attorney. It was decided he would defend me. We ended up having an indigency hearing. We had to prove we could not afford to hire a paid attorney for Kara. It was agreed that Lester Moore would remain my attorney and Kara would have a public defender. June Riley was appointed as the federal public defender for Kara at our hearing in April.

Later, we had our meeting with Lester Moore. Kara went with me, but he asked her to step out of the room. He explained he was now my attorney and some things had to be left unsaid in front of Kara. We would encounter this strange situation when Kara went to see June and I was asked to step out of the room. It seemed utterly ridiculous to us. There seemed to be some fear that we might end up cutting separate deals and testifying against each other. How could we testify against each other? We had done nothing wrong! Besides, didn't they realize we were telling each other everything we discussed in those private attorney meetings? We thought the attorneys were both insane!

CHAPTER 20

LIFE DRAGS ON

Over the next few weeks, the probation officers did drop by the house. My probation officer was a skinny, wimpy-looking man. He went through everything. He looked in every drawer, in the closets, and under the beds, and he even went up in the attic. Kara's probation officer sat on the couch with Kara and drank coffee and commented on what a lovely house we had and what a good housekeeper Kara was. It was quite a contrast.

Back in March, Paul and Jen and Kara and I had resumed an old tradition we had started back in the 1970s when we first started coaching football together. We went out to eat and to the movies every Tuesday night. We came to love those Tuesday nights. We felt safe and secure in the darkness of the theaters. Going out to those movies and to eat was the only time we really enjoyed ourselves socially while we were out on bond. Paul usually insisted he pay for everything on Tuesday night. It was equally important that we always met at one of our homes and rode together in the same car. We laughed a lot that spring. Those Tuesday nights were like healing medicine for Kara and me.

In April, we continued to make our court dates. There were court dates to exchange discovery, court dates to ask for more time, and as mentioned, court dates to appoint Kara's lawyer, June Riley. We discovered just how slowly the wheels of justice turned. We continued to make regular trips back home to Rector, Arkansas. In fact, we went every week or at least every other week. My parents' home was a sanctuary for us. We completely quit going to visit our friends, and they never stopped by or called us. Maybe I am using the term *friends* too liberally.

All through April, the drug tests continued. I was called in almost weekly for a "random" drug test. I was being tested at least three or four times a month. Kara was never called in for a random test.

Most of April, it seemed we spent being called back into court at the federal building for one thing or another. We were spending a fortune just parking downtown at eight dollars a time.

We continued with the Tuesday night movie schedule with Paul and Jen. The rest of the week we usually rented movies and lived in a dark house with no lights on, the blinds pulled shut, and the car parked behind the house.

Byron Smith continued calling on the phone from prison. He called almost every night. He needed a friend. He was lonely. I would be there for him. I continued to send both Will and Byron money each week, as I had promised. Will was still at Mason, and Byron was finishing up at FCI Memphis.

As for our friends in Memphis, Arkansas, and Missouri, they never called or wrote a letter or anything. Our family, however, grew closer. We needed all their love and support, and they willingly gave it.

The trial date continued to be moved back. It was moved back from May till June and then from June to July. Discovery continued to change hands. The more serious hearings of suppression and other items would be held later. The waiting was wearing on us. We were quickly reaching the point that we just wanted to get it over with. On the other hand, each time it was postponed, it meant we had more time together. It was a trade-off.

CHAPTER 21

BYRON SOUTH AND A NEW JOB

Byron informed us in April that he would be released from FCI Memphis on May 6, 1998. His mother lived in Tupelo, Mississippi, but she had already told him she would not come to pick him up. She owned a large dog food company and several federal compresses (large warehouses where cotton was stored) across Mississippi. She was very wealthy. It was surprising because there was not one indication from Byron that he came from a wealthy family. His mother lived on a street that had only two homes: hers and her sister's. The name of the street was South Road. Apparently, his dad was dead.

Byron must have burned his mom in the past. She told him he could stay at her house only long enough to get a job and get out on his own. She told him to ride the bus to Tupelo and she would pick him up at the bus station. He had told me he had a brother in Memphis, but they had not even spoken in years.

Later in April, in one of his phone calls, he said they were going to give him only fifty-three dollars when he left the Memphis prison. It was about twenty miles from the prison to the bus station downtown. If he called a cab, and it was too far to walk, he wouldn't have enough for a bus ticket to Tupelo when he got to the bus station. He told the officers at prison, "What am I supposed to do? You've given me just about enough money to buy a cheap handgun on the street and rob a liquor store so I'll have enough money to buy a bus ticket to Tupelo."

Eventually, he talked them into giving him about one hundred dollars, but I agreed to pick him up at the prison when he got released on May 6. I told him he could stay at my house if he needed to. He wanted to do that at least for a few days.

He was released midweek. I waited in the parking lot and picked him up when he came out. He had on street clothes they had given him and a few toiletries. We went to the mall, and he bought a couple pairs of jeans, two pairs of socks, and two colored T-shirts. I bought him a few packages of underwear. We went to the house, and he called his mother to tell her he was out and staying at our house. He gave her our phone number and address. She agreed to send him a couple hundred dollars via Western Union. She told him he would have to pay her back.

He picked up the money at a Western Union outlet in a nearby Kroger Grocery Store. We went to a shoe store, and he purchased some work boots and a decent pair of tennis shoes. We ate a buffet meal at Pizza Hut. It was all you could eat, and eat he did!

My mom and dad continued to experience failing health. They began staying for about two weeks at a time at Paul's and then would return home to Rector for a week. It became increasingly obvious that they could no longer take care of themselves. It would just be a matter of time before they would move into Paul's for constant care.

By the end of the second week in May, Byron had a driver's license and had secured an interview for a job with a company in North Mississippi. I drove him to Southaven for an interview with ABC Construction Company. They were interviewing him for a job driving a bulldozer. They offered him the job starting Monday. They said they would pay him nineteen dollars an hour and he would have full medical benefits. They did not care at all that he was an ex-felon. They told him to be at work at 6:30 a.m. the next Monday morning. They said they were clearing land to build a multimillion-square-foot warehouse.

I began driving him to work every morning. We had to leave the house at 5:30 a.m. to get him to work on time. He worked until dark, caught a ride to a nearby quick shop, and called me to come get him. He was working seven days a week (about ninety hours). He was promised a raise to twenty-two dollars an hour if things worked out the first month.

Kara and I began to work our schedule around Byron's. Kara got up and cooked him breakfast at about 5:00 a.m. each day. We didn't eat supper until around 9:00 p.m., after I had driven over and picked him up after work. Because he was working seven days a week, this became quite a grind for us. He was bringing home well over one thousand a week.

At some point, he suggested I might as well just get a job with the same company since I was going to and from various job sites anyway. I was still getting paid by the school system, but Kara wasn't working. He said he had heard one of the surveyors needed a helper. He told me he would point out the man to me the next day when I took him to work. He pointed out the truck that belonged to the surveyor, and I went over and introduced myself and talked to him about the job. He did need a helper. I found myself at the office filling out the paperwork and agreeing to take the job. I already had medical benefits with the school, but now I had duplicate benefits. I would start at nine dollars an hour and be raised to eleven dollars per hour after one month. We would be working six days a week and sometimes seven. I would end up averaging about ninety hours a week myself. I soon discovered I was making more money at my new job than I was making at my school job. My income had increased more than 100 percent. It would sure help our finances.

It proved to be hard work. I had a radio, two sledge hammers, two bags of wooden stacks, flags, and a hard hat and steel-toed boots. I was walking over fifteen miles a day. We were rarely in the shade, and it was hot! We drank gallons and gallons of Gatorade every day.

The man I worked with told me he was surprised I stayed with it. He said men half my age quit because of the heat and the hard work. I told him I had grown up picking cotton. There was no harder work than picking cotton. I enjoyed the solitude of the work, the physicality of it, and the extra money it provided. It seemed to be therapeutic.

I did have to leave the job on occasion for scheduled or random drug screens with the probation officer. The company was completely accommodating in that regard. However, in looking back, I think I made a mistake. I believe I should have spent every possible moment with Kara and the family. I didn't realize it at the time, and now it is only in hindsight. There was no way I could have known that at the time.

In June, Byron picked up a car a from a mechanic friend of his at Atoka, Tennessee. All of a sudden, he didn't need me to take him or pick him up any more. He was happy, but I was happier. We seldom worked at the same job site. His car would help me too.

MAY—JUNE 1998

Our legal situation was never far from us. We continued to meet with our attorneys. The meetings were usually to review additional discovery from the government or for us to provide our attorneys with more positive evidence. We tried to gather up every scrap of evidence that might help our case.

In addition, we had several court dates in May, in which more time was requested and granted to bring June Riley up to speed. We also met an investigator from her office that could help us in our case. Lester Moore thought that was great. He said we needed an investigator. Since we didn't have the money to hire one, it was nice to have one assigned to our case that we didn't have to pay. He came from the public defender's office.

Our drug testing also continued. They seldom scheduled our tests on the same day, so it was taking two or three trips for the scheduled tests. I was having random tests about once every three weeks. With the time missed from work, gas to get there, and eight dollars to park, it was costing us one hundred dollars a month just to make it to those tests and the court dates.

The trial date was moved to July. That would later be canceled because of vacation time for the AUSA, Terry Descussio. It was then scheduled for August 3, 1998.

In June, we finally had a suppression hearing. We tried to suppress the statement Kara had made in the bedroom because she was never given her Miranda rights. I wanted to challenge the search warrant. The house, the barn, the woods, and the two cars had all been searched multiple times before the search warrant was presented to me. The photographs taken by Sergeant Lewis were clearly taken in the morning hours of July 13, 1997. I tried to tell Lester it was sunshiny that morning and started raining around 12:30 p.m. I told him Lewis's photos would show the sun was shining and there would probably be clocks in the house in his photographs. I argued that the other photographs and the videotape were both shot in the afternoon while it was raining. I told him they had searched before the first set and before the second set was taken. The search warrant didn't get there until the videotaping was finished. The search was clearly illegal. I showed Lester the warrant hadn't been signed until 2:40 p.m. at Judge Chriss's house.

I had a very heated argument with Lester about the search warrant. He told me, "If we try to suppress it, it will make us look weak."

I replied, "I don't care how we *look*. We need to do everything we can to win. The search warrant was bogus."

He convinced me that if we were going to trial, we didn't want to look weak. I never understood his reason or logic. We did not try to suppress the warrant.

I didn't just have a problem with the time of the warrant but I also had a problem with the custody of evidence. I noticed on the back of the search warrant, there was a place for an officer to fill out regarding checking the evidence into the appropriate evidence room of the arresting authority. In this case, it would have been the evidence room of the general sessions court where Judge Chriss served. He was the signing authority on the warrant. That section was left entirely blank. I wondered why. I was so surprised by that fact that I placed a call to that evidence room and asked if evidence had ever been logged into it. It had never been logged into that evidence room. That seemed like a big mistake regarding chain of custody of the evidence.

It became clear that the federal authorities, Agent March and his bunch, had seized the evidence. I am sure it had been logged into a federal evidence room somewhere. However, a federal judge had *not* signed the warrant. What that meant to me was that the chain of custody of the evidence had been illegally broken. The evidence should have been logged into the general sessions court's evidence room and then logged out by the federal authorities and logged into their evidence room. Clearly (at least to me) the federal authorities had no right to seize evidence obtained on a state warrant. Our attorneys agreed, but neither of them did anything about it. The search warrant and all the seized evidence was allowed to stand despite the irregularities. Kara and I were both furious that our attorneys were not mounting a more vigorous defense. We felt like they were ignoring the fact that we had rights, even as accused people.

CHAPTER 23

JULY INTO AUGUST: READY FOR TRIAL

I continued working, and Kara continued to manage the house and take care of me, Ricky Short, and Byron South. Feeding three men and herself required quite a bit of planning. Every other week or so, one or both of the men would pay for the groceries. I was able to pay off a lot of our credit card debt as I worked the surveyor's assistant job and still received my pay from the school. Of course, the school pay would run out at the end of July. We were still scheduled to go to trial August 3, 1998. I began trying to save a little money.

The surveyor I worked with was a retired navy man. We shot boundary lines, building sites, parking lots, curbs, and even on-property roads and driveways. He wanted to train me to survey. The work was interesting. He said the company would provide me with a truck and I could earn more that $120,000 a year. That was about four times more than I was making teaching school. I explained to him if I was acquitted, I would go back to Shelby County schools. I wanted to continue teaching and coaching. If I was found guilty, then none of it mattered anyway. I would be going to jail. The work continued to be therapeutic for me, but Kara was left at home all day to worry about our situation.

About the only legal matter we had to deal with was to provide the court with a list of witnesses we planned to call. Some of them would have to be reimbursed in order for them to attend and testify at the trial.

By the end of July, we had a houseful of people. Our daughter, Mary Lynn, and her family were there, Byron South and Ricky Short were there, and Allen and Renee and their two-year-old daughter and newborn baby were there. We fixed pallets on the floor and made arrangements where everyone would sleep. My mom and dad had moved into Paul and Jen's and would stay there throughout most of the trial.

It was nice to be surrounded by friends and family that cared. However, Kara and I were nearing the breaking point. It had been more than a year. The pressure was really getting to us. We often needed to be alone. It was hard to concentrate on anything. Everyone had advice for us, some of it good and some bad. All in all, everyone around us knew we were innocent and encouraged us and tried to keep our spirits up. It was hard.

As trial date rolled around, we became even more anxious. I mean, anxious in the sense that we needed closure. We had carried this burden now for thirteen months. The stress was remarkable. I had lost almost twenty pounds, most of it from worry and lack of sleep. It wasn't unusual for Kara and me (one or both of us) to wake up at 2:00 a.m. or 3:00 a.m. and not be able to go back to sleep. My working had helped. On many workdays, I was so exhausted I collapsed in bed or fell asleep watching one of our rented movies.

I had reviewed every scrap of evidence the government had turned over. Some of the evidence they had turned over was totally absurd. They had page after page of some people's names they had evidently taken out of a filing cabinet in one of the spare bedrooms. The sheets all looked as follows, with only slight changes to the names by the numbers:

100 Max, Larry, Ann, Mary
200 John, Larry, Ann, Susan
400 James, Steve, Carole, Carolyn
800 Andy, Courtland, Patricia, Jenny
1600 Jeff, Carl, Sherry, Lisa
3200 Jeff, Carl, Sherry, Lisa

400R Max, Larry, John, Thomas/
Ann, Mary, Susan, Carole
800R Max, John, Thomas, Steve/
Mary, Susan, Candice, Paula
1600R Max, Larry, John, Thomas/
Mary, Susan, June, Carole
3200R Jeff, Carl, Sam, Carlton/
Sherry, Lisa, Barb, Suzanne
110H Courland, Mike, Jennifer, Tara
330H Courtland, Mike, Jennifer, Tara
ST Pat, Dick, Shirley, Evelyn
Dis Pat, Dick, Shirley, Evelyn
HJ DeAngelo, Wayne, Heather, Nikki
LJ DeAngelo, Wayne, Heather, Nikki
PV DeAngelo, Wayne

I couldn't imagine what the government thought they had with these lists. Lester Moore said the government thought they were financial/drug records. These were mostly recorded in small pocket notebooks and dated. These were really what track coaches call poop sheets. They were sheets that we passed out to our athletes before track meets so they would know what events they were participating in. The 100, 200, and 400 were all dashes. The 800, 1600, and 3200 were distance races. The 400R, 800R, 1600R, and 3200R were all relay races. The 110H and 300H were hurdle races. The ST, DIS, HJ, LJ, and PV were all the field events (shot, discus, high jump, long jump, pole vault). It was laughable they imagined these to be important documents.

The discovery also included statements given by Sam Nance. There were multiple statements, and all of them were contradictory. For instance, Sam Nance said the following:

In September 1997: "I don't know nothing about no fire in Memphis."

In October 1997: "I heard Jack Phillips was cooking meth and caught a building on fire."

In December 1997: "I hear Jack Phillips and Phil Roseburg were cooking meth and caught a building on fire.

On January 27, 1998: "Me and Timmy Tisdale was cooking meth in a barn in Memphis. I scraped off some sodium metal from a bar into an ether solution. I guess I made a mistake. It caused a small explosion and set the barn on fire."

In that January statement, he also said Kara and I were running errands and buying supplies for them. He said we were preparing the pills in the house (he called it making "flea powder") for them to use to cook in the barn.

We weren't worried about any of these statements. We were puzzled, though, about which statement he would testify was the truth at the trial. All of these were sworn depositions given to law enforcement officials. It was quite obvious he was a liar. We felt more confident that whatever he said could easily be impeached.

Strangely enough, there was no statement from Timmy Tisdale. He was on the witness list, but maybe he had told the truth—that is, that we had nothing to do with the fire or the cook. Since we received no information about what he might or might not have said, we had no way to prepare for his testimony prior to the trial.

Their witness list was long. We only recognized the names of Nance, Tisdale, and three or four of the officers/agents we had met. We assumed the rest were probably other law enforcement personnel or firemen.

There were no fingerprint reports, which was surprising to us. They had threatened to fingerprint everything. Apparently, they had fingerprinted nothing at all. They had listed as evidence things taken from the house, like coffee filters and aluminum foil. We could not figure out how any of that could possibly be real evidence.

Most of what they had seized and had tested had proven to be just regular household items, like grease and salt—nothing at all significant. They had found a small glass pipe and three or four marijuana roaches in a cellophane wrapper in a junk drawer. I had taken those out of a backpack that belonged to one of my children's friends in 1994. I was surprised it was still even around. We were not charged with those items.

About the only meth-related evidence were the Walmart pill receipts they had taken from the house. There were five or six of these receipts. Each receipt showed there were four to six packages of pseudoephedrine allergy tablets on each receipt. The receipts were from Walmart stores in Southaven, Mississippi, and nearby stores on Shelby Drive (near the Mississippi state line) in Southeast Memphis. We lived clear across town in Northeast Memphis. There were probably fifteen Walmart stores between our house and those stores. Kara worked at a Walmart near our house, but there were no receipts from her store or any of the stores near our house.

In fact, the dates on all but one of these receipts were the very dates we were in the Days' Inn in Fultondale, Alabama. We were nowhere near Southaven, Mississippi, or Shelby Drive in Memphis, Tennessee, on those dates. Sam Nance had a grandmother that lived in Southaven. He went to her house frequently to mow the grass, do small repairs, or just to visit. He was only minutes away from the store on Shelby Drive in Memphis. Rarely did he go to the casino in Mississippi without mentioning that he had to go by and see his grandmother in Southaven.

According to the discovery, those receipts were found on the TV, on the kitchen cabinet, and in one of the spare bedrooms. Ricky Short told us the receipt dated from April of 1997 and found in the bedroom where he slept was his. He worked at his brother's pallet company. His elderly uncle ran a government program for new state prison releases. It was a work program. The men worked making pallets for the pallet company and were paid a fair wage. They worked in an enclosed area. Ricky said he kept allergy pills in his truck not only for him but also for the workers who had allergies that were set off by the sawdust. Because of the dates on the receipts and the time of purchases, we weren't worried at all about them either.

The only disturbing evidence in the discovery were statements allegedly made by Kara and me. There was at least a kernel of truth in them, in that we were at least talking about the subject they reported.

However, we didn't recognize the four or five things they claimed we had admitted. Because there was no factual basis to these claims, we weren't overly concerned about them. They just made us angry.

All in all, we felt confident. If all they had on us was what was in the evidence they had turned over in discovery, we had nothing to worry about. We were ready for trial. We wanted nothing more than to put it all behind us and work on restoring our tarnished reputations.

Saturday night, August 1, just before bedtime, Ricky Short asked me if I would step outside for a minute. He wanted to talk to me privately. He had something he wanted and needed to tell me.

We went out the front door and sat down on the front porch steps. He looked at me and said, "Jack, there's something I need to tell you. I should have told you before." I told him to go ahead.

Ricky said, "You know, I told you about the Shelby County deputy that pulled up in front of the house early that Saturday morning the day before the fire on Sunday. The one I saw when I was buttoning up my shirt and looking out the front window."

I said, "Yeah."

"There's more to the story," he said. "Jack, a few minutes after the deputy left, I went out to get in my truck to go to work. It was parked right in front of the barn almost, you know, where I usually park to stay out of everyone's way."

"Yes," I said.

He continued, "It wasn't quite daybreak yet, and when I started to get in my truck, I heard a voice say, 'Ricky, what are you doing?' I almost jumped out of my skin! The voice came out of the dark barn. About that time, Sam Nance came out of the barn. He asked me what the cop was doing there. He had a big pistol in his hand. I told him I had no idea what the cop was doing there."

I asked Ricky why he hadn't told me this before now. He said, "Because Sam told me it would be better for me if I forgot I ever saw him there. He told me particularly not to tell you he had been there. Jack, I went to school with him. I know him. He was threatening me with the pistol. That's why I left and didn't come back until the middle of the next week. I've been carrying this around with me all these months. I'm sorry I haven't told you about it before. I was just afraid to tell you."

I told Ricky, "You'll have to come to court Monday morning and talk to Lester Moore. You get to the courthouse before 9:00 a.m. Also, you go in the house and write all this down, just like you told me, word for word. Don't leave anything out."

It seemed to me we now had another important piece of evidence. We had already planned on calling Ricky as a witness. Now, he would really have something to talk about. There were twists and turns everywhere. I had no idea what might happen next.

CHAPTER 24

TRIAL DAY 1:
MONDAY, AUGUST 3, 1998

We met our attorneys in the hallway just outside the court-room where the trial would be held. Ricky Short had met with Lester Moore and June Riley and given an affidavit about Sam Nance and the gun. We drove ourselves to the trial that first day and parked across Front Street in the parking garage we had always used. We paid the eight dollars to park.

The surprise came when we parked, walked down an enclosed stairwell to the street below, and stepped out on the sidewalk to cross Front Street. There was a small entourage of press waiting for us. We felt like we had been ambushed. Cameras began snapping pictures, and we had questions being shouted at us and microphones being stuck in our faces. Between the crowd of press and the traffic on Front Street, we were stuck. We couldn't get through the crowd. Lester Moore had told us not to speak to the press, so we tried to ignore everything around us. Some of the questions were insulting and demeaning, like if I sold drugs to kids at school. It was hard not to respond. The TV cameramen were the worst. When we tried to step around them, they just moved and blocked our path. We were stymied and could not move.

Paul and Jen came along from somewhere, and Paul grabbed both of us and physically pushed us through the crowd. It was extremely physical. We felt physically threatened, but Paul rose to the occasion. We determined that this would be the last and only time we would drive ourselves to the federal building. We could not imagine going through this every day. When we got inside the federal building, we asked and were shown some obscure entrance on the other side of the building that we could use. From that time on, we rode downtown with Paul and Jen and had them drop us off several blocks from the federal building. We could approach on foot from several directions and enter the building unnoticed. We were never discovered entering or leaving the building again by the press. The still shots they had taken that first morning would be used in the *Commercial Appeal* the next day and on several occasions after that. The TV video was used to introduce our story many times on the local news stations. Paul and Jen would pick us up on a street corner about two blocks from the federal house after our trial each day.

At 9:00 a.m., we were ushered into the courtroom. Our attorneys directed us to the defense table. At the government's table sat Terry Descussio, the assistant United States attorney, and DEA agent Mike March. They whispered together, sneered at me, and seemed to be laughing at us and mocking us. It seemed low-class and unprofessional. It was typical of their behavior throughout the trial.

At about 9:15 a.m., Lester Moore and June Riley told Kara and me to follow them. We went out of the courtroom, down the hall, and found a quiet alcove. Lester said the government had offered us a deal. Even though we had said from the beginning we were innocent and would never plead guilty, we were both anxious to hear their proposal.

Lester said, "Jack, here it is. If you will plead guilty, they will let Kara go."

Kara blurted out, "No way! No way, Jack! There's no way Jack is pleading guilty to something he didn't do!"

I told Kara, "Just a minute, Kara. Go ahead, Lester. Finish what you were saying."

Lester said, "They only arrested Kara to get you to plead guilty."

I said, "I know. How much time are they talking about for me to do?"

He said, "Two hundred sixty-two months to life."

I was stunned. Was he serious? He had told me I could possibly get up to 10 years (120 months) if I went to trial and was found guilty. Now he was telling me the government wanted me to plead guilty to over 20 years to life for something I didn't do?

Kara went ballistic. "No way, Jack! No way!"

I told her to wait a minute. I asked Lester if we could think it over and give them an answer tomorrow. He said he would check, and he left to ask the AUSA.

Kara exploded, "Jack, you're not pleading guilty!"

I told her, "Kara, just listen. I didn't say I would plead guilty. I just want to buy some time for us to think about it. After all, I would die for you. You do understand that if we go to trial and are convicted, we're going to *prison*! Not county jail. *Real prison*. The only way I would ever consider pleading guilty is to keep you out of prison. Just wait, Kara. Let's buy some time. We'll talk about it tonight, at home."

Lester returned and said, "You have until 9:00 a.m. tomorrow. Let's go in. The judge is ready."

At 9:48 a.m., Judge Jason T. Burns entered the courtroom, and it all started. The first order of business was jury selection. This process is called voir dire. The court weeds out some of the prospective jurors, and each side, prosecution and defense, can challenge and eliminate up to three jurors for cause. We would choose twelve jurors and two alternates.

I guess I was most surprised by how much Lester and June deferred to Kara and me. As each juror answered basic background questions from the judge, the government, or our attorneys, they turned to Kara and me and said, "Well, what do you think?"

I was surprised they were even asking us. I knew how important the makeup of the jury would be. Kara and I knew nothing about picking a jury. Didn't they do this all the time? Weren't they the professionals? Shouldn't they make these decisions? They wanted us to respond on each juror as if we were the experts.

There were a couple of wealthy Germantown businessmen in their late sixties in the jury pool. They lived in the most affluent suburb in the Memphis area. They would be educated and conservative. I didn't think they would be open-minded in any drug case. I said as much. Besides, they both admitted they had read quite a bit about the case and seen all the newscasts on TV. We used two of our challenges on these men.

Our jury ended up being mostly female (eleven), including the two alternates. There was only one male. He worked for Coca Cola. I felt like he might be fair. Another juror I liked was an anthropology professor at Memphis State University. One black female was seventy-nine years old. Others were mixed racially and mostly in their mid- to late fifties. I didn't know if we had a good jury or not. Why our attorneys had deferred to us was still an unanswered question.

The prosecution began his opening statement. For the first time, we were given an idea of the case they would present against us. Here are some of the highlights:

- Jack Phillips provided the sodium metal used in the cooks. He ordered it through Bartlett High School where he worked.
- Kara Phillips provided the ether [we are not clear where she got it from].
- There were actually five cooks in the barn; one in 1994, one in 1995, one in May of 1996, one in May of 1997, and one the day of the fire, July 13, 1997.
- At these five cooks approximately 11 pounds of meth was produced.
- At each of these cooks, the Phillips were present and running errands, buying supplies, preparing pills (flea powder) in the house, and Kara was washing dishes and cooking meals for Nance and Tisdale.
- Jack Phillips once sold a pound of meth to someone in Mississippi for $16,000. He gave Nance and Tisdale $8,000, but he never paid them the other $8,000 he owed them.

- Jack and Kara Phillips purchased thousands of pills for the cooks.
- The day of the fire, Jack Phillips tried to prevent the firemen from entering the barn.

These were just some of the outlandish statements made by the AUSA in his opening statement he made to the jury. Not one of the abovementioned items was actually true. We simply couldn't believe they were making all these false allegations. There was no way they could prove any of this because it wasn't true. Most of this was absolutely new information to us. We were stunned and angry. Was this a kangaroo court? There was simply no way these allegations could be proven.

Our opening statement was that we were hardworking, law-abiding citizens, with no drug problems and no extra money. We were just working-class people doing our jobs and trying to get by. It was stressed we were not in town when these cooks occurred.

The testimony began with firemen. They basically testified when they arrived that a white male was spraying water on the barn with two garden hoses. They told him to get out of the way, and he did. He told them, they said, something about the stairs being bad. Not one of the firemen could identify Jack Phillips as being that white male they saw when asked on cross-examination.

The day ended at 5:30 p.m. Paul and Lester walked us out into the hallway. TV and print journalists blocked our way. TV camera lights came on, and we were bathed in bright lights. Microphones were stuck in our faces, and questions were shouted in our direction.

Lester and Paul cleared a path to the elevators. One of the female reporters got on the elevator with us. After all, it was a public elevator. She never said a word, but she was listening in case we did. We never spoke either.

There was a larger crowd waiting for us outside the building. Again, Paul pushed us through all the reporters and across the street until we reached our car.

We followed Paul and Jen to their house. My mom and dad were there, and we went in and caught them up on all the proceedings. We also showed them a copy of the affidavit Ricky Short had given to the attorneys.

Before we left to go home, we called our house, and our daughter, Mary Lynn, answered the phone. We asked what they were doing for supper, and she said, "Waiting for you and Mom to get home." We decided to stop at Steak Escape and pick up some sandwiches and french fries on the way home. We took everyone's order over the phone. The meal cost us over forty dollars.

We reached home and rehashed the day's events. Everyone was curious as to what had happened. Before we knew it, it was bedtime. We were both exhausted and slept soundly. We would be up early the next morning for day 2.

TRIAL DAY 2: TUESDAY, AUGUST 4, 1998

F irst thing Tuesday morning, I informed Lester Moore I would not accept the government plea deal and plead guilty to this crime for so much time. I asked him if there could be a counteroffer for less time? He said, "No, that was their final offer." Kara and I had talked about it all night. She was adamant that I should not plead guilty.

The government continued to present its case against us on Tuesday. They were bringing in the officers that were on the scene the day of the fire.

The first witness was Sergeant Lewis of the Shelby County Sheriff's Department. He was the officer going around snapping pictures the morning of the fire. Sergeant Lewis was an older black gentleman with graying hair and a soft demeanor. He identified himself as "the ranking officer on the scene until that afternoon." He was ambiguous as to when the crime scene became the responsibility of the DEA (Drug Enforcement Agency).

This was also the first opportunity for the government to present its visual evidence in the form of the photographs taken by Sergeant Lewis. There were several notable facts concerning the photographs and the accompanying testimony of this officer. Here are just a few:

1. Sergeant Lewis testified he took the photographs personally.
2. In the photographs, he shot coffee filters, Reynolds Wrap, jars of liquid (grease) taken from above the stove, lists of the names of the track team participants we mentioned earlier (taken from the filing cabinet in the spare bedroom), the cellophane wrapper with the glass pipe, and three marijuana roaches. He said he laid the cellophane on the bedroom dresser and took the photograph. There was a bumper sticker laying on the dresser that said Do the Crime, Do Hard Time.
3. He photographed a track coach's blank starter pistol still in its marked box, which was located in the utility room.
4. Sergeant Lewis testified he had searched the woods, the barn, the cars, and the house prior to taking the pictures.
5. He testified he started taking the photographs around 11:00 a.m. and finished shortly after noon.
6. He took a photograph of our Camaro with the hatchback raised and the Walmart pill receipts for the allergy pills lined up neatly in the back of the car.
7. From clothes hanging out of the drawers and closets to the boxes on the floor, it was obvious the house had been searched prior to the photographs being taken. Sergeant Lewis confirmed this again.

Sergeant Lewis verified all the above facts when cross-examined by Lester Moore. Lester particularly emphasized the fact that Sergeant Lewis had searched prior to taking the photographs. Since the search warrant wasn't signed until 2:40 p.m., the times of the search were an obvious problem. Furthermore, the weather during this photo shoot proved beyond a shadow of a doubt that they were taken prior to 12:30 p.m. According to the National Weather Service, it was raining by 12:30 p.m. It was a clear, sunny July morning during the time Sergeant Lewis took his photographs. It was not raining. Since it rained all afternoon after it started, it was proof positive he took the photos in the morning as he said.

As Lester was cross-examining Sergeant Lewis, Judge Burns suddenly sprang to life. He called for a sidebar with all the attorneys.

He addressed Lester primarily but included June Riley in his rebuke. He said, "You can't bring up the search warrant now. You should have done that at the suppression hearing."

Lester said, "I know, Your Honor. I'm just getting the times verified for the record for future appeals."

"Very well," the judge said, "but don't question the search warrant in front of the jury. Do you understand?"

"Yes, Your Honor," Lester replied.

In regard to the bumper sticker, Lester said to Sergeant Lewis, "What about that bumper sticker? The Phillips have pretty-nice bedroom furniture. Was that bumper sticker stuck on their dresser?"

Sergeant Lewis said, "It was just there. I don't know if it was stuck on there or not. I just laid the cellophane right there with it."

Lester said, "Do you know who put it there?"

"I do not," the Sergeant said.

The bumper sticker was highly inflammatory. In fact, it was on the walls about eye level all around the courthouse cafeteria, where the jury ate their meals. It was extremely prejudicial. Kara and I realized there was nothing sacred and no such thing as fair play.

Sergeant Lewis also photographed a couple of propane tanks. They had been put into one of the small pump house structures where we kept the lawnmower and several containers of gasoline. It would later be claimed that these tanks contained something other than propane, something they used in manufacturing meth. There was never any real proof that this was a fact, just an allegation that was dangled out there because the valve had turned a bluish green on a couple of them. They were not my tanks—I knew that. They had said they would take fingerprints on these tanks. We never heard of any fingerprinting or fingerprint results. We actually believe there were fingerprints on these tanks, but because they were not ours, they were never introduced.

In addition, two female Shelby County deputies testified. One of the ladies, Bonita Thream, said she worked in the warrant office of the sheriff's office. Jane Ashby was a patrolwoman. These women admitted they were the two female officers that strip-searched Kara in our bathroom the day of the fire. The testimony was that they were looking for needle tracks to see if Kara was a meth junkie. Kara was fifteen to twenty pounds overweight. It was obvious she was no meth addict.

Bonita Thream never claimed she brought a search warrant with her. However, we had our suspicions. Sergeant Lewis was adamant that he had a search warrant to search that morning even though the active search warrant wasn't signed until 2:40 p.m. Was there a previous warrant? Was that previous warrant flawed? Did they need a second warrant (the 2:40 p.m. warrant) that wasn't flawed and would better fit their need? We've never been able to ascertain that.

The other officer, Jane Ashby, testified she took the videotape of the evidence the afternoon of the fire. This too, like the first set of photographs, was shown to the jury. She told the court another officer accompanied her and took a second set of still photographs. The jury also saw the second set of still photographs.

There was a particular problem with the video. The AUSA, Terry Descussio, told the jury there was about a ten-minute parking lot surveillance on the front of the videotape. He was clear it had nothing to do with our case. They played it in front of the jury. The jury was required to sit through a meaningless ten minutes of surveillance. The video began taping at 2:41 p.m. according to the time on the tape and clocks in the house. It was clear they were using a dirty tape. It was a tape that was recorded over something else. This was a federal criminal case being tried in a federal court. Surely, a dirty tape like this could not be used as evidence. But it was.

Officer Ashby did a voice-over on the tape as she was videoing. She narrated everything she videotaped. She stated the time was 2:41 p.m. She started outside the house under an umbrella during a driving thunderstorm. As she proceeded through the house, there were clocks in every room. It was easy to track the time. In one frame, she videotaped us in the den. I was on the floor turned sideway and leaning back against the recliner. I was trying to relieve the discomfort in my bad shoulders from having my hands handcuffed behind my back for so long. It showed Kara handcuffed and sitting in the other chair.

In the utility room, she took the lid off the box that held the starter's pistol. She placed the lid underneath the box. She laid a rag over the end of the pistol to cover up the orange plug that plugged the barrel of the starter's pistol. She said on the videotape, "It looks like we have found a pistol in the utility room." I don't know what she did with the box of blanks that were in the box with the pistol. In fact, this starter pistol had my name, Coach Phillips, engraved on the wooden handle. It had been given to me by my track teams at the spring athletic banquet.

This was another attempt to prejudice the jury. The fact of the matter was that I had sold my only two guns, two shotguns used for hunting, at a yard sale in 1990. I had not owned a gun since that yard sale.

It was also obvious that additional searches had occurred. The items in the rooms had changed. Some had been stuffed back into drawers, and other drawers had things hanging out of them. Things just weren't the same as they were in the photographs taken that morning. In every room, a person could easily see it had been tossed. It was also obvious the first set of photographs had been taken in the morning before the thunderstorms hit. In the morning pictures, the sun was shining. In the afternoon video and second set of pictures, it was storming and raining.

Also, our bedroom was an interesting place in the second set of photos and the videotape. The bumper sticker, which had caused such an uproar when reviewing the first set of photographs, was no longer on the dresser. In the second set of photos and the videotape, either the bumper sticker had been removed if it was actually stuck to the dresser or the bumper sticker had simply been removed if it had only been laid on the dresser for the first set of photographs. Either way, someone was tampering with evidence. The female officer said she knew nothing about any bumper sticker and never saw one on the dresser (remember, Sergeant Lewis knew nothing about the bumper sticker either).

The video ended around 3:10 p.m., and so did the taking of the second set of photographs. At least that was the last time we saw them videotaping and snapping photos. They had also photographed things in the woods, in the barn, in the cars, and the yard. Both sets also recorded a shaving kit in the backyard. It was on the back side of the Camaro. Inside the shaving kit were prescription bottles, gloves, goggles, and other assorted items. The name on the prescription bottles was Timmy Tisdale.

We broke for lunch, and testimony started up again after lunch. The first officer to testify was Shelby County detective Will Smart. He was Detective Martin's partner. It was clear that Martin was the lead detective in this partnership. He definitely seemed to be in control of the house the day of the fire. It was when Martin and Smart left the scene that DEA Agent March took over. It was Smart and Martin that left to go get the search warrant. That search warrant was presented to me (placed on the end table) at 3:15 p.m. or so that afternoon.

I really suspect the sixty-five grams of meth found in the amazing bucket was planted. I believe if it was, then it was brought to the scene by one of both of these detectives. I fully believe the bucket that was used was the same bucket that I had seen months before laying in the garbage dump at the edge of the woods. I believe they brought meth to the scene, placed it in the bucket, and used it to prove the lab in the fire was a functioning meth lab.

It was Detective Martin that could not explain the audiotape. He could not clarify why the loaded question they had asked me was not on the tape. The point right up to where they asked me that question and I asked for an attorney was not on the audiotape when it was played in court. The authorities read me my rights (twice) afterward when I again agreed to talk. They even mentioned the reason for reading me my rights again was because I had agreed to talk again after previously asking for an attorney. His only explanation was that "maybe the tape recorder had been knocked off the table."

There was also a dispute about who actually controlled the crime scene, the Shelby County Sheriff's Department or the DEA? At what time did control swap hands? No one seemed to be able to say. It was clear by the time Martin and Smart left the scene that DEA Agent March had been in control. The afternoon session ended about 4:50 p.m. with Detective Martin still on the stand.

Kara and I had ridden to court that day with Paul and Jen. They had let us out about three blocks from the courthouse, and we had walked on in and entered through the obscure side door. We left the same way, walked two or three blocks, and waited on the corner for them to pick us up.

Again we rode with them to their house. After visiting with Mom and Dad, we called Mary Lynn and told her to order pizza for everyone. We told her there was money in our dresser to pay for it. We went to the movies that night with Paul and Jen. We ate at the movies and rushed home and went to bed early.

My routine in the courtroom was to carry my Bible inside my briefcase. I read my Bible during much of the trial. Lester wanted me to take notes and pass information to him, but every time I did, he basically told me "Shush." At some point, I quit trying to talk to him at all. I only talked when he asked me something or when something outlandish happened. Then, I made him listen to me. June was proving to be totally useless. Her investigator was worse.

On that Tuesday morning, our investigator was in the hallway outside the courtroom mingling with our witnesses. At some point, he began telling them, "If Jack and Kara beat this, one of you will pay for this! You better remember, if Jack and Kara go free, someone in this hallway will be convicted and go to jail."

Our own investigator was intimidating our witnesses! At lunch, several of them told me what he was saying earlier. We told Lester and June about it. They ask for a sidebar with the judge and the AUSA. The judge called up the investigator and asked him about it. He didn't deny it. The judge banned him from the courtroom and all federal property around it until the trial was over unless we called him to testify as a witness. We were not going to do that. We never saw him again.

TRIAL DAY 3: WEDNESDAY, AUGUST 5, 1998 (PART 1)

This would be the most pivotal day of the government's proof against us in this case. We again rode with Paul and Jen and avoided the press completely. The court was called into session at 9:07 a.m. Detective Martin was still on the stand.

His testimony centered 'round going to Judge Chriss's house that Sunday afternoon to have the search warrant signed. The times he was giving just weren't jelling. Smart had testified they had driven east from our house to an office in Midtown Memphis. Smart testified that he personally typed the search warrant. He would have had to have driven from out east, typed the warrant, driven to the judge's house in another part of the city, explained the need for the warrant, gotten it signed, and driven all the way back to our house in less than two hours. It was impossible to complete the driving alone on a perfect day in that length of time. That Sunday afternoon, there was a driving thunderstorm. That time frame just did not allow enough time to type the warrant and sit around and explain the need for it to the judge. It didn't add up.

Lester Moore had done a good job of pointing out the time discrepancy in this testimony. Overnight, the government had figured out how to straighten this out. Detective Martin simply testified that he, Martin, had just called in the search warrant and had someone else type it. They just dropped by the office and picked it up. No, Smart did not type the search warrant—someone just working in the office that Sunday afternoon actually typed it.

Detective Martin was also rather vague as to when the search warrant arrived at the property in question. He just said he couldn't remember. That was supposed to be good enough.

The government's next witness was an employee of Walmart whose purpose was to explain what the pill receipts said. He also testified about the store codes (to identify the store) and the dates on the receipts. A fireman testified next. He verified there were fifty to sixty empty John Deere ether cans upstairs in the lab.

Another witness that morning was a Shelby County deputy that testified he found hundreds of empty blister packets in the burn barrel behind the barn. Later, there would be a portrayal of there being hundreds of thousands of blister packets in that barrel.

The stars of the day to testify on day 3 was coming up next. Sam Nance and Timmy Tisdale would testify before the day was over. Their testimony would prove to be hard to listen to because there was very little truth in the testimony of either.

CHAPTER 27

TRIAL DAY 3: WEDNESDAY, AUGUST 5, 1998 (PART 2)

S am Nance approached the witness stand and was sworn in. He was clean-shaven and had a fresh haircut. He looked like the proverbial boy next door. The AUSA had done a remarkable job trying to make Sam Nance look presentable. He also did a remarkable job in trying to link Sam Nance and Jack Phillips together.

Through leading questions and innuendo, he made it sound like I had been Sam Nance's high school football coach. The questioning and testimony went something like this:

AUSA: Now, Mr. Nance, you and Jack Phillips and Kara Phillips are from the same home town, is that correct?

Nance: Yes, Rector, Arkansas.

AUSA: Now Mr. Phillips was a big sports person in Rector, Arkansas and his wife was a cheerleader, right?

Nance: Yes. She was a cheerleader and Jack was a sports hero in our town. He was the quarterback on the football team and an All State basketball player. I think he played some college and pro baseball, too. He was a legend.

AUSA: And you were an athlete, too? A football player?

Nance: Yes.

AUSA: So you and Jack were pretty close.

Nance: Yeah.

AUSA: So, you were a football player and he was a...your coach, right?

Nance: Yeah, that's right.

AUSA: Were you involved with cooking meth at 711 Highway 72 in Bartlett, Tennessee?

Nance: Yes.

AUSA: So how did Jack and Kara Phillips involve you in cooking meth?

Nance: Jack said a guy named Depriest had showed him how to cook meth. He asked me if I wanted to cook meth in a barn at his house.

AUSA: Did you agree?

Nance: Yes.

AUSA: How many times did you cook meth there?

Nance: About five times.

AUSA: When was that Mr. Nance?

Nance: Once in 1994, once in 1995, in May of 1996, in May of 1997, and the day of the fire in July 1997.

AUSA: Was Jack Phillips present...were Jack and Kara Phillips present when you cooked meth at the barn?

Nance: Yes, they were both there.

AUSA: What role did the Phillips play?

Nance: Jack got the sodium metal we needed. He got it through Bartlett High School where he worked. Kara got the ether, but I don't know where she got it. They both bought pills and made flea powder out of the pills in the house. Kara washed dishes and cooked meals for us, too.

AUSA: Now you said you cooked meth with them there five times, is that right?

Nance: Right.

AUSA: How much did you cook? Let me ask it this way... How much did you cook in 1994?

Nance: About one pound.

AUSA: About how much did you cook at the cook in 1995?

Nance: Two pounds.

AUSA: How about May of 1996?

Nance: A pound. About one pound.

AUSA: How much did you cook in May of 1997?

Nance: Two pounds.

AUSA: How much meth were you cooking in July of 1997 the day of the fire?

Nance: We were going to cook five pounds.

AUSA: Now let me see that is:

1994 one pound
1995 two pounds
May 1996 one pound
May 1997 two pounds
July 1997 five pounds

That would be a total of eleven (11) pounds. Is that about right?

Nance: Yea, that's right.

AUSA: Did the Phillips ever sell dope for you, Mr. Nance?

Nance: Yea, Jack sold a pound of meth to somebody in Mississippi. I don't know who, for $16,000.

AUSA: What happened to the money?

Nance: Jack brought $8,000 to me and Timmy. He was supposed to collect the rest of the money and give it to us. He never did. He still owes us $8,000.

AUSA: Did he keep the money?

Nance: I don't know if he kept the money or he just never collected it. All I know is we didn't get our money.

At that point, Lester Moore began to cross examine Sam Nance. He asked him why he was currently in jail, and Sam told him for cooking meth in Cape Girardeau, Missouri. Lester asked him about his prior arrests, and Nance replied, "This is the first time I've ever been arrested or convicted of a crime."

Lester then asked him about what happened the day of the fire. Nance's testimony was truly astonishing, considering what he had previously stated in sworn depositions.

Nance: Me and Timmy Tisdale and a guy named R. A. Boone was cooking meth in the barn. I got tired and went downstairs to the bottom floor of the barn and fell asleep on a broken down couch for a couple of hours. Timmy went in the house and went to sleep on the couch in the house. R.A. was cooking and did something…you know, made a mistake and caused the fire. He came running down the stairs and told me to get up there because there was a fire. I ran upstairs and looked but it was already out of control. I grabbed some of the containers we was using and threw them out a window. It was getting hot, so me and R.A. got out. We got downstairs and I grabbed a 55 gallon drum of alcohol and put it in R.A.'s truck. I ran in the back door of the house and woke Timmy up and told him to come on; we had to get out of there because the barn was on fire. Timmy and me got on our motorcycles and got out of there. We circled around to a McDonald's, grabbed some food, and then circled around behind a field across the highway and watched the fire. We saw the firemen and the police start showing up. The barn was really burning and putting out a lot of smoke. We watched for a while and then headed back home.

Moore: Where were the Phillips?

Nance: They were in the house cooking up pills when the fire started.

Moore: Had they been there all weekend?

Nance: Yeah.

Moore: What were they doing all weekend?

Nance: Running errands and buyin' pills and cookin' them up and stuff.

Moore: What about the other cooks? Were the Phillips there, too?

Nance: It was just me, Timmy, Kara, and Jack. Sometimes one of the guys living there might have been home. I am not sure.

Moore: Like who?

Nance: I'm not sure.

Moore: Mr. Nance, did you testify a moment ago that when the fire started you woke Timmy Tisdale and you and him went across the highway behind some field and watched the fire?

Nance: Yeah.

Moore: You also testified about cooking, what was it…?

One pound in 1994

Two pounds in 1995

One pound in May 1996

Two pounds in May 1997

Is that right?

Nance: Yeah.

Moore: What happened to all that meth?

Nance: Me and Timmy took it and sold it back home in Arkansas and Southeast Missouri. We also did some of it.

Moore: You mean you used it yourselves?

Nance: Yes.

Moore: And in July, the day of the fire, you were cooking five pounds?

Nance: Yes.

Moore: Did you?

Nance: No, it all burned up before we made the meth.

Moore: Mr. Nance, if you and Tisdale took all the dope and sold it or did it yourselves, what did the Phillips get?

Nance: (long pause)…We told them they could scrape the jars.

Moore: Scrape the jars! Are you kidding? Didn't you say Mr. Phillips sold one of the pounds for $16,000? That's a lot of money. For the meth you said you cooked, there's a lot of money involved. The Phillips have nothing. Are you telling me they let you do this, and they were satisfied with "scraping the jars?"

Nance: I don't know.

At this point, Lester Moore began reading off a whole list of alternate statements Nance had given in previous sworn statements to law enforcement officials. At one point, he asked Nance about sixteen specific and contradictory statements he was reported to have sworn to in those depositions. He adamantly denied making each—all sixteen! Most of these sixteen statements were made to another DEA agent. When the defense tried to locate the DEA agent, we found he had been transferred and reassigned and was working in South America. During lunch, we subpoenaed him. He would be flown back to the United States and later testify as a defense witness in regard to these statements.

In all the sworn statements Sam Nance had given, he had never mentioned R. A. Boone before. In fact, he had previously explained how he, Sam Nance, had messed up and started the fire. Although I didn't personally know R. A. Boone, I had played basketball against him back in the sixties. I also knew he had married and divorced a girl from my hometown that I had graduated from high school with. He had attended high school about thirty miles from my hometown.

Even more remarkable to me was how Sam Nance could be asleep in the barn and testify about what was going on in the house—like Timmy Tisdale being asleep on the couch and Kara and I cooking pills. If he was really asleep in the barn, how could he possibly know what was going on inside the house? That testimony should not have been allowed, but neither of our attorneys objected to it because they didn't catch the impossibility of it. They didn't want to hear anything from me about it either.

The dates and amounts cooked at each alleged cook would only be based on testimony by Sam Nance. No one else verified the dates or the amounts. Timmy Tisdale would testify later there was a cook in May 1997. That was the only verification of date or amount. In regard to the alleged five pounds being cooked the day of the fire, Nance testified no meth was actually cooked because the fire started and burned up the mixture before it became meth. If that is true, and it was testified to and accepted as true, then where did the sixty-five grams of meth in the amazing Shadrach, Meshach, and Abednego bucket that would not burn come from? Furthermore, if they were cooking five pounds, they must have invested thousands of dollars in the supplies. It was inconceivable they would take twenty-five dollars to thirty dollars worth of alcohol and leave behind six thousand dollars worth of meth in the bucket. The meth could have been placed in the cab of the truck or even hung from the handlebars of the motorcycle. Were we to believe they left that and took the giant drum of alcohol that would be clearly visible in the back of a pickup truck fleeing from a meth lab fire? By the way, no one saw a red pickup truck leave the scene of the fire.

Furthermore, despite the fact that Sam Nance had admitted cooking meth at this location five times, he was not charged with manufacturing meth or any other crime in relation to these events. Nance continued to vehemently deny he had a deal with the government. Terry Descussio, the AUSA, joined in that denial, claiming that Nance had been promised nothing for his testimony. It was obvious to me he had immunity. That in itself constituted a deal. However, we could not get Nance or Descussio to admit to such an obvious fact. Sam Nance was dismissed as a witness.

CHAPTER 28

TRIAL DAY 3: WEDNESDAY, AUGUST 5, 1998 (PART 3)

The next witness the government called was Timmy Tisdale. He too testified he had no immunity and no deal with the government. Just like Nance, however, he was not charged with any crime connected to these events. AUSA Descussio assured the judge, jury, and defense that he had no deal either. He did not testify to drug amounts and only to the May 1997 cook and the July 13, 1997, cook (day of the fire). His testimony went as follows:

1. He testified he met Jack Phillips in October or November of 1996. He met Kara Phillips in early 1997. He said he met Jack in Arkansas and it had nothing to do with drugs.
2. He testified when the fire started, he was asleep on the couch inside the house. He said he had come in the back door of the house and the back door was unlocked. He said he looked down the hall and saw Jack Phillips alone and asleep in the bed. He said he did not see Kara Phillips. He said Sam Nance had awakened him and told him to get up and move because there was a fire. He admitted dropping his shaving kit in the backyard in his haste to get away.
3. He said Jack never woke up.

4. He said Sam Nance was asleep in the barn downstairs and R. A. Boone was cooking meth upstairs in the barn when the fire started.
5. He said at the May of 1997 cook, he and Sam Nance had set up and cooked meth on a Friday night and left. He said the Phillips were not at home. He testified they were out of town at an athletic event.
6. He said the Phillips had not been home during the weekend of the fire in July. He said they had come home unexpectedly early that Sunday morning before daylight.
7. He never testified to any amounts.

Under cross-examination, he admitted that earlier that spring, Jack and Kara Phillips had saved his marriage by counseling with him and his wife, Donna. Lester Moore asked him to read the front of the card he had sent to Mr. and Mrs. Phillips in October of 1997. As he read the card, a large tear rolled down the side of Tisdale's face. He couldn't look at us after that. He claimed he had no deal and had been promised nothing for his testimony. He also testified he had never been arrested or convicted of a crime prior to the one he was serving time for (the meth cook in Cape Girardeau, Missouri).

Under cross-examination, Lester Moore made a big deal about the fact the government claimed Tisdale had never given a statement and we had nothing to go on as to what he might testify about. We could not prepare a proper cross-examination when we didn't know what he might say. Lester claimed we were being ambushed by his testimony.

After his testimony, Lester told me, "Jack, he really doesn't want to hurt you or Kara. He's just saying what they told him to say."

I knew it was true. Tisdale didn't want to hurt us. He claimed he was just doing his time in jail and didn't expect to get anything for his testimony. I knew that was a lie. Again, it was obvious he had immunity. I also knew he had been arrested in Caruthersville, Missouri, for marijuana once and cocaine once. He had told me that himself.

At least he had admitted we had not been home for the cook(s). He, like Nance, had testified about events occurring in the barn while he slept in the house. Again, our lawyers apparently didn't catch it. That testimony, like Nance's, was illogical.

In regard to the May 1997 cook, he had testified truthfully that we were not there and were out of town at an athletic event. Kara and I were in Chattanooga, Tennessee. I was coaching in the state track meet the last weekend in May.

CHAPTER 29

TRIAL DAY 3: WEDNESDAY, AUGUST 5, 1998 (PART 4)

The next witness was interesting and completely unknown to us. His name was Stanley Richardson. He was an insurance agent with an agency just down the road from our house. He said about 8:30 a.m. on the morning of July 13, 1997, he was driving by our house on his way to McDonald's further down the highway. As he passed the house, he said he saw a tremendous amount of smoke that seemed to be coming from the rear of an old barn on the property. As he was gawking at the fire, he said he saw two white motorcycles speed out of the driveway right in front of his car. He said they accelerated to a speed up to maybe ninety miles per hour. He said the bikes ran a red light at Kate Bond Road. He got caught at the same traffic light on red.

As he sat there, he watched the motorcycles reach Germantown Road and then peel off in different directions. The light change,d and he drove about a half a block and turned left into McDonald's. He said as he was parking when the motorcycles circled by and parked on the other side of the restaurant. As he went in one side door, the two bike riders came in a side door across the restaurant from him. They ended up standing next to one another in line. He said he asked them, "Was that barn on fire back there?" He said they replied, "No, we were just burning some trash in a barrel behind the barn."

He said he got his order, ate his breakfast, read the sports page, and prepared to go open his office at 9:00 a.m.

As he came by the house on his way to the office at about 8:55 a.m., he saw the flames coming out the top of the barn, the fire trucks and police cars were everywhere. He said a lot of people had pulled to the side of the busy highway to watch and there were a lot of people in the front yard of the house. He parked his car and walked across three lanes of traffic, the median, then three more lanes of traffic to reach the side of the road where the house and barn were located. He asked for an officer, and a man that identified himself as a DEA agent met him, listened to his story, and took his business card. He said he had told them about the two men on the motorcycles that were obviously running from the scene of the fire.

At that, the court adjourned for lunch. We went to a nearby diner with Paul and Jen. We were all furious with the testimony of the morning. It was just one lie after another. The falsehoods of Sam Nance and the AUSA, Terry Descussio, were ridiculous. We couldn't believe the AUSA would allow such lying.

When court resumed, it was already 2:30 p.m. The next witness was the Shelby County sheriff's deputy that had been called to the scene the day before the fire by the jogger. That was on July 12, 1997. This officer testified the jogger had told him he smelled chemical smells in front of that property. He said he went to the property, parked out front, got out of his car, and looked around. He said he did not smell anything or see anything out of the ordinary. He said he was probably there about five minutes. He said he wrote up a report about it and gave it no further thought until he saw the fire on TV the next day. He did not know Sam Nance was in the barn armed with a pistol and watching him. I wondered what might have happened if he had come onto the property near the barn?

The last witness that would be called that day was DEA agent Mike March. The thrust of his testimony was that there was a meth lab and Kara and I were guilty. While he was on the stand, the government again showed both sets of photographs and the videotape. This was the second showing of the visual evidence.

March did admit that he and his partner had questioned Kara in the bedroom the day of the fire without Mirandarizing her. He said we had dropped by their office the next day on our way to Arkansas anyway and turned in a list of all the people we knew who owned motorcycles. He said that proved we were willing to talk, so it didn't really matter if they read Kara her Miranda rights or not.

He also said that while we were in their offices on July 14, 1997, we admitted buying pills and supplies for Nance. He said they had sprung the evidence of the receipts on us and we had freaked out. He went on to say it was obvious we were heavily involved in this cooking operation.

His testimony parroted what Detective Martin had said. He identified and elaborated on all the things in the pictures and the video that showed all the containers and that they were lying in the edge of the woods and behind the barn on the ground. He pointed out the plastic containers that had hoses coming out of the tops (handmade hoses). He identified the blister packets and claimed there were not hundreds but tens of thousands of them. He pointed out the blue/green substance on the valves of the propane tanks and indicated that meant they contained some substance used in the manufacture of meth (he said the tanks were empty but that was a residue of that substance on the valves).

AUSA Descussio also got March to testify about the insurance salesman, Stanley Richardson, that had given him the business card that morning and told him about the motorcycles and riders that fled the scene. This created a little problem for March. He had testified he didn't get there until after lunch. Now we saw he was admitting he was there at 8:55 a.m. Our lawyers did not challenge him on the time.

It had gotten late. It was 5:20 p.m. The court finally adjourned for the day. It had been grueling for us. We had heard the worst of the accusations against us. It was hard to watch people we had never harmed try to do harm to us. We just didn't understand how it could be happening to us. It was painful that the AUSA and his officers were twisting, distorting, manipulating, and creating the "truth" (so-called) in order to convict us. We were hurt and angry and tired.

On the elevator going down, Lester Moore turned to me and said, "Jack, you need to prepare a list of our witnesses and what they can testify to. The government will rest tomorrow, and we will start presenting our case."

I looked at Lester and said, "Lester, I gave a book to you with all that in it six months ago! It had twenty-seven witnesses and all they could testify about. Where is the book? Have you not even read it? It contains our side of the story. Where's the book, Lester?"

He said, "I don't know. I guess I lost it."

I went crazy. I growled at him, "How could you lose it? You've never even read it! You've never even talked to our witnesses, and the trial is half over! You don't even know our side of the story. You lost it? Are you kidding me?" It was 5:40 p.m. He wanted me to prepare a book overnight that had taken me weeks to prepare before when I had nothing to do.

"I'm sorry, Jack," he said has he moved passed the open elevator doors into the hallway. June just scurried after him, staring at the floor.

Kara and I both felt like crying. How painful. Our own attorneys had not prepared to properly defend us. Paul and Jen picked us up three blocks from the courthouse. We drove across town to Paul's house. We sat down and told Mom and Dad everything that had happened. I was animated talking about Lester Moore and his request I make a book with all my witnesses and what they could testify to. Mom went to her purse and pulled out a hardback green appointment book. She had purchased it for her beauty shop. She grabbed my hand and said, "Take this, Jack. Go on home and write it all down again, honey. That's all you can do."

I said, "I know, Mom. Thanks."

Kara and I went home to the houseful of people. They were all there to help, but we could have used some peace and quiet and time and space. I finished writing in the book at 5:00 a.m. It was just beginning to break dawn. It was now Thursday, August 6, 1997.

CHAPTER 30

TRIAL DAY 4: THURSDAY, AUGUST 6, 1998

Court was called back in session at 9:36 a.m. DEA Agent Mike March was still on the stand. He resumed his testimony. The AUSA led him through the discovery of the silver ball and the sodium metal inside, the test kit explosion, and had him explain about the sixty-five grams of meth he had found in the bucket that wouldn't burn and couldn't be filled with water no matter how many gallons of water the firemen sprayed on the fire. It also had indestructible methamphetamine in it. The meth wouldn't melt and couldn't be destroyed by the water sprayed on the fire or in the bucket (or so they would have us believe). His testimony lasted about thirty minutes before Lester Moore began to expose Agent March for what he really was.

Lester began his cross-examination about 10:00 a.m. The cross was magnificent. Agent March was on the defensive from the get-go. It was clear Lester was comfortable on his feet in a courtroom. June also crossed March, but she didn't add anything to our cause one way or the other. That was true not only on this cross-examination but it was true throughout the entire trial.

At one point, Lester returned to the defense table and retrieved a document from his satchel. He asked March the following questions:

Moore: What time did you get to the scene?

March: About 1:00 PM.

Moore: How could that be true if Mr. Richardson gave you his business card at the scene around 9:00 AM?

March: I don't know. I didn't get there until about 1:00 PM.

Moore: Agent March, did you tell the grand jury you had investigated and found evidence that Jack and Kara Phillips had purchased 600 cases of pseudoephedrine pills for Nance and Tisdale to use to cook meth?

March: I did.

Moore: Did you in fact investigate and find evidence that Jack and Kara Phillips had purchased 600 cases of pills?

March: Yes sir, I investigated.

Moore: (looking at Agent March and smiling and slightly raising his voice) Did you investigate and *find evidence* the Phillips purchased 600 cases of pills? You heard the question Agent March!

March: No sir!

Moore: Did you investigate and find evidence that Jack and/or Kara Phillips ever purchased ONE case of pills?

March: No.

Moore: In the last 13 months you have been investigating Jack and Kara Phillips have you found any evidence they ever committed a felony?

March: No.

Moore: Then why did you tell the grand jury they purchased 600 cases of pills?

March: I miss spoke.

Lester Moore wasn't finished with Agent March yet. He still had a few questions to ask him:

Moore: Agent March, you heard Mr. Nance's testimony that Jack and Kara Phillips were in Memphis all weekend the weekend of the fire, right?

March: Yes, I heard that.

Moore: You must know that Mr. and Mrs. Phillips claim they were not in town, right?

March: Yes.

Moore: Were Jack and Kara Phillips in Memphis the weekend of the fire as Nance testified or were they out of town like they claimed?

March: No, they were not in Memphis that weekend.

Moore: Where were they?

March: They were in room #206 of the Days' Inn in Fultondale, Alabama.

Moore: What time did they check out?

March: 11:55 a.m. on Saturday, July 12, 1997.

Moore: How do you know where they were?

March: I checked and verified it myself.

Moore: Did they come straight back to Memphis when they left the Birmingham suburb?

March: I don't know.

Moore: Isn't it true Agent March that you do know. Isn't it true they have gas receipts for Saturday afternoon in Nashville. In fact, don't they have an Exxon gas receipt that shows they were in Nashville Saturday night as late as 10:30 p.m.?

March: Yeah.

Moore: Well, did they go straight home from Birmingham to Memphis?

March: No.

Moore: Didn't they even have a gas receipt from Oak Grove, Kentucky on Saturday, July 12, 1997 at about 6:00 p.m.?

March: Yes.

Moore: Agent March, you personally checked out their motel receipt and all of these gas receipts, didn't you?

March: Yes.

At this point, Lester changed the course of direction again. Here's the next round of questioning in the cross-examination of DEA agent Mike March:

Moore: Agent March, you are aware of the conflicting statements Sam Nance made in his sworn depositions, are you not?

March: Yes, there are some inconsistencies.

Moore: On January 27, 1998 didn't Sam Nance swear in a detailed statement about how the fire started?

March: I believe he did.

Moore: Didn't he state in that sworn deposition that he and Timmy Tisdale were cooking meth when the fire started?

March: Yes, he did.

Moore: Yet you heard his testimony yesterday that he was asleep when the fire started. He said Tisdale was asleep in the house. He testified a guy named R.A. Boone was cooking the meth when the fire started. Did you hear him testify to that, Agent March?

March: Yes, I heard it.

Moore: Well, Agent March, do you have any idea which version is the truth? Was it R.A. Boone or Sam Nance and Timmy Tisdale cooking the meth when the fire started?

March: I don't know. I guess it was R.A. Boone.

Moore: You don't really know do you? Do you really think it was R. A. Boone?

At this point, Judge Burns interrupted the cross-examination of Agent March. He apologized for the interruption, but he had a question for Agent March.

Judge: Agent March let me ask you something. Where is this R.A. Boone? His name keeps coming up. There has been testimony that he was the one cooking the meth when the fire started. I haven't heard from him or seen him. He is not on the government's witness list. Where is R.A. Boone?

March: We can't find him, Your Honor.

Moore: Judge, if I may ask a question.

Judge: Go ahead, Mr. Moore.

Moore: Agent March, have you looked for him?

March: No.

Moore: Isn't that why you can't find him. You haven't even looked for him?

Judge: Asked and answered, Mr. Moore. Move along.

Moore: Yes, Your Honor. Agent March, let me ask you about the video in use here. In fact, let me ask you about the video and the audio recording as well, and even, the alleged statements reportedly given by Jack and Kara Phillips at your office the day after the fire, okay?

March: Okay.

Moore: On the video tape there is a surveillance scene on the front of that video, you know the one the government has already played twice for the jury, isn't that right?

March: Yes.

Moore: Did that surveillance scene have anything at all to do with this case?

March: No sir, it did not and we explained that both times we showed it.

Moore: Yes, you did. My question is how did that get on this tape?

March: I guess it was on there before it was used to video anything in this case.

Moore: You mean you used a "dirty" video? Do you mean someone just grabbed a video tape that had already been used and just taped over it?

March: I guess.

Moore: Is that a normal thing to do in a federal criminal case? This is a federal criminal case. Would you really do that in *any* case?

March: No.

Moore: Why did that happen here?

March: I don't know.

Moore: You should know Agent March, you used that tape.

Your Honor, I would like to introduce a letter from Mr. Jim French, an audio-visual specialist often used by this court for the government. He has examined both the audio and video tapes and he says both tapes are "dirty." Both tapes have been taped over. He says these tapes could have been erased and manipulated in any number of ways and no one could detect it because they have so much recorded information underneath what we hear and see.

Judge: Please place this as Exhibit A for the defense.

Lester Moore did not tell Judge Burns the rest of the story. Jim French had called Kara and me on a Friday night and said he had mailed a letter that was certified and would explain everything he had found concerning the audio and videotapes. He said on the phone they should have never been used.

On Sunday afternoon, Jim French, 5 feet 9 inches and 145 pounds and only 48 years old, fell dead with a heart attack while walking down the hallway of his home. He had never smoked nor drank and had no history of heart problems or disease. He actually died before we received the certified letter from him that he had sent.

Lester continued with Agent March:

Moore: Agent March, you heard Nance and Tisdale both testify they had no "deal" with the government, right? That they had not been promised anything?

March: Yeah, I heard that.

Moore: Well, what do you say?

March: I wouldn't know. I know I didn't promise them anything.

Moore: Maybe not, but Jack and Kara Phillips are the only ones charged.

Do you know why Sam Nance, Timmy Tisdale, and R.A. Boone are not charged?

March: No sir, I don't.

Moore: One more thing, Agent March. You said Jack and Kara Phillips both admitted at your office that they bought pills for Nance and Tisdale, is that right?

March: That's right.

Moore: Did you record those statements?

March: No.

Moore: Surely you took notes of that meeting?

March: No.

Moore: In all your training, Agent March, at Quantico and other places, aren't you always taught to use a clean tape in a case?

March: Yes.

Moore: But that didn't happen here, did it?

March: No.

Moore: Aren't you always told to record statements or at least take notes to preserve all the facts and keep the evidence clear and accurate?

March: Yes.

Moore: One last thing, Agent March. You repeatedly threatened Jack and Kara Phillips with the idea you were going to take fingerprints on everything. Yet, I didn't see one fingerprint report in the discovery. Why is that? Are there any fingerprint reports on anything?

March: No sir. Not to my knowledge.

Moore: You said you were going to didn't you, Agent March?

March: Yes, but in an investigation we are allowed to lie to the suspects if necessary to get the truth.

Moore: So there were no fingerprints taken?

March: Not to my knowledge.

June Riley followed up with a few repetitive questions. Then Descussio, the AUSA, rose for redirect. He tried to refocus the situation.

AUSA: Agent March, just a few follow up questions. How much drug paraphernalia was lying in plain view at the edge of the woods and behind the barn?

March: Quite a bit.

AUSA: Was it easy to see with the naked eye?

March: Oh yes.

AUSA: Who lived in the house then?

March: Jack and Kara Phillips.

AUSA: Could they have lived there and not seen all that meth cooking stuff lying around?

March: No way.

AUSA: No more questions, Your Honor.

The government's last witness was a lady from the FBI crime lab in Miami, Florida. Since there was no fingerprint evidence, she really didn't have anything much to report. She didn't comment on the sixty-five grams of meth in the bucket either.

The government rested its case against Jack and Kara Phillips at 2:54 p.m. Both defendants, through their attorneys, ask for a directed verdict of not guilty on the basis that the government had not proven its case. It was granted in the case of Kara as to count 3 (maintaining an established meth cooking lab) and that charge was dropped. Counts 1 and 2 on Kara and all three counts on Jack were maintained.

At eight forty-five that morning, Lester Moore had met with our witnesses. All twenty-seven of them were present. The meeting lasted a little less than fifteen minutes. It was the first time Lester or June had met with any of our witnesses (except Ricky Short, when he gave them the affidavit about Nance and the gun earlier in the week). They had both also met Paul, of course. By the time court had started that morning, neither Lester nor June had read our witness book that I had stayed up all night preparing.

Lester basically told our witnesses he wouldn't be calling but about one-third of them. He told them to tell the truth. He also advised them to go slow on cross-examination. He said they should think through their answer no matter how long it took before they answered any questions from the AUSA. He also said, "If you don't know, there's nothing wrong with saying 'I don't know.'"

It was 3:37 p.m. and time for us to mount our defense. There would be three witnesses this afternoon: Paul Phillips, my brother; Andrew Logan, a student from my high school; and Diana Smith, also one of my students.

Paul's testimony was riveting. He was at our house several times each week and at different times of the day and night. He often just dropped by unannounced on his way here or there. He and I talked on the phone every day and saw each other on a daily basis too. We were close. He told the court, "If Jack is guilty, you might as well arrest me too, because Jack couldn't be guilty unless I am guilty too."

He also mentioned that he came by my house either the last week of May or the first week of June and saw some vehicles there he didn't recognize. He knew the people that had been staying at my house then and what kind of vehicle each of them drove. He said these were vehicles he had not seen before. Kara and I had not only gone to Chattanooga for the state track meet but we had taken a vacation to Florida the week following that—the first week of June 1997. He told the court he mentioned this to me when I had called him from Florida. He said I told him it was probably some other people with troubles coming to live at my house. Jack said he had called several times and talked to Ricky Short or Byron South, and they had both assured him everything was fine at home as far as they knew.

Andy Logan told the court how I routinely gave all my lunch money away each day at school. He said kids with no money for lunch were always coming to me and I would give them the last dollar I had. He told the court how I would put my unlisted phone number on the board and beg the students to call me to come get them if they were somewhere driving or riding in a car with someone who was drinking and driving. I told them I would stay home the nights of Homecoming, Valentine's Day dances, prom, etc.—anytime there was a major school function. Andy said he had dropped by our house several times himself and always been welcomed by Mrs. Phillips and Coach. He said he came by often to get advice on college choices or problems he might be having at home or at work.

He said every student at our school (and it was the largest high school in Tennessee) knew they were always welcomed at the Phillips' house.

Diane Smith said about the same thing. She had been on the girls' track team. In her case, there was a special bond because her senior year, her parents went through an ugly divorce. Her older sister had been in Jack's class too but had graduated. She was off to college. Diane was home and felt the brunt of the divorce. She felt like her parents were pulling her in different directions. She said, "Coach Phillips was my lifeline. He and Mrs. Phillips helped me so much. He wasn't just my track coach, he was my friend. He counseled with me all the way through the divorce. I spent many afternoons and nights at the Phillips' house."

Court adjourned at 4:06 p.m. Our attorneys told us to stick around for a few minutes. We agreed to meet Paul and Jen on our street corner in about thirty minutes. Considering all that had occurred in our life up to that point, the next twenty minutes were some of the strangest minutes we would ever see.

We were all four still seated at the defense table—from right to left were Lester, me, Kara, and June Riley. Kara and I were both leaned back in our chairs. Lester and June were both leaned up on the table, looking at one another. They seemed to be really animated, and the discussion turned first as to whether either Kara or I should testify. Kara and I had already discussed the possibility. We felt like Kara should not testify, for sure. We didn't want Terry Descussio messing with her, confusing her, upsetting her, and twisting her words. We had not decided if I should or should not testify. We told this to the attorneys.

I think June and Lester were in total agreement that Kara should not testify. It seemed like June kind of thought I should, but Lester didn't think I should.

Lester said, "Jack, Terry Descussio is counting on you testifying. He wants you to. He knows you are a teacher and has the impression you are pretty articulate. He thinks the confidence you have in speaking is the very weakness and noose he'll hang you with."

I said, "Lester, I can handle the AUSA."

He said, "No, you can't. He's been doing this for twenty-five years. He is a real pro. He will drag you up to a mudhole then use your own words to throw you right over into the middle of it. You'll never see it coming. Listen, they haven't proven one thing against either of you. There's absolutely no evidence against you, Jack. They don't have a case. Their only hope is to trip you up on the stand."

I could hardly believe what I was hearing. Not that the government hadn't proved a thing and had no case. We knew that all along. The shocking thing was the look in Lester Moore's eyes and June Riley's eyes. Even the tone of their voices was startling. I had a real epiphany at that moment.

I slapped the table and said, "Wait a minute, Lester. You and June are looking at us differently. You're speaking to us differently. You're treating us as if we are *really* innocent! You're even being more respectful to us. The tone of your voice is more respectable when you speak to us. I see it all over your faces! You have never truly believed we were innocent this entire time until today when the government rested its case. Now you see for sure we are innocent! June, you're doing the same thing with Kara and me too. Our own lawyers, and you haven't believed us until today. Thirteen months, Lester! Six months, June! Shame on you both! You never believed us, and now you believe because the government couldn't prove the case!"

Lester tried to speak, so I put a finger in his face and said, "Don't you say a word! Don't you dare try to deny it! It's so obvious." Lester and June both just hung their heads to hide the embarrassed looks on their faces.

I told him, "I'll probably not testify. I will probably take your advice. I think it is obvious to everyone in the courtroom we are innocent."

We left the court that day wiser and more educated about lawyers, even our own. I couldn't wait to see the family. They all agreed I should not testify except for Jen, Paul's wife. She said, "Jack, you should testify. The jury needs to hear from your own lips that you are innocent. Terry Descussio will not get to you. You can handle him."

CHAPTER 31

TRIAL DAY 5: FRIDAY, AUGUST 7, 1998

The court was called to order at 9:38 a.m. The first person we called was DEA agent James Rodriguez. He had flown in from South America. He was the agent that had taken one of the sworn depositions from Sam Nance.

He took the stand, and Lester read him the same sixteen statements Nance had made in the sworn deposition but contradicted during his testimony. Actually, he just denied making the statements at all—the same sixteen questions Nance had denied making under oath. Agent Rodriguez confirmed Nance had sworn under oath to tell the truth in that deposition taken by Agent Rodriguez. He said Nance did, in fact, utter every single answer that Lester read and attributed to Nance.

Lester asked him, "If Sam Nance said he didn't say those things, would he be telling the truth, Agent Rodriguez?"

Agent Rodriguez said, "No, he would not."

There was no cross-examination, and Agent Rodriguez was dismissed as a witness. He had served his purpose. He had proven that Sam Nance had lied under oath either when giving the deposition or at trial.

The next three people we called would all have lived at our home between October of 1996 and July 13, 1997, the day of the fire. They had been there at different times and for various durations.

The three were all magnificent. They credited Kara and I with literally saving their lives. The AUSA didn't bother to cross-examine any of them. I was a little surprised Lester didn't ask Ricky Short about the affidavit and Nance with the gun the day before the fire. I would have thought that was important enough to have Ricky testify to the facts of that event.

We also called Carl Person. He was the track athlete I coached at the state track meet in May. He was also the track athlete that took up the money from his teammates and bought the starter's pistol for me with my name engraved on the handle. He presented the gift to me at the athletic banquet the preceding spring. He was eloquent from the stand and very poised just like he was competing on the track and in the jumps in the field events. I was so proud of Carl.

Lester called our last witness. It was Brother John Henson. However, some problem arose with his testimony. For some reason, he was not allowed to testify about the conversation we had in the teachers' lounge at my school in March of 1997. That was the conversation in which he told me, "When you bring those people with problems into your home, their problems have a way of becoming your problems and landing on your doorstep." He did testify that he lived right around the corner from us and passed our house every day. He told how he stopped in to see us unannounced. He testified he had known us for thirty years and had married us in 1970, and that we had good character.

June called one witness. She called Kara's sister, Mandy. Mandy had stayed at our home many, many times. Sometimes she stayed for as long as a week on each trip. She often traveled from New Orleans (where she lived) to Arkansas and Missouri. She traveled often by Amtrak or we drove to New Orleans to pick her up. Sometimes we took her back to New Orleans by car. She and Kara were really close. She testified she was absolutely sure we had nothing to do with drugs at all.

The defense rested. All that was left were the closing arguments. The verdict would come after that.

TRIAL DAY 5: FRIDAY, AUGUST 7, 1998 (PART 2)

Terry Descussio, the AUSA, went first with his closing argument. He showed all the photos and the videotape to the jury again for the third time. He played the audio recording for the jury for the second time. He emphasized the stuff at the edge of the woods and in the backyard behind the barn and concluded that we had to have known what was going on. There was no way all that could be there and we wouldn't know. He said he knew the witnesses weren't the most solid citizens, but they told the truth. Jack and Kara Phillips were in partnership with them in the meth-manufacturing enterprise. He hit on the receipts too. He said we had been in our car a lot that weekend and the pills' receipts in our car proved we were, indeed, buying pills for the cooks. As far as the people living at our house that testified, he said truthfully they were probably involved as well.

Finally, it was our turn. Now, Lester Moore would have the jury read the inside of the card Tisdale had sent to us. He could point out in the card where Tisdale said that Nance had planned on *lying*. He could remind the jury the pills' receipts were found in the house and not in the car, as they had portrayed. He could point out the inconsistencies in Nance's and Tisdale's testimony in court. They couldn't even agree if we were in Memphis or not. He could point out to the jury that I could not have purchased the sodium metal bars through Bartlett High School because I never in my life worked at Bartlett High School. My brother Paul had worked there, but not me. He could point out that Kara could not have washed dishes or cooked meals for them while they cooked meth in the barn because they only cooked meth in the barn when we were out of town. We weren't within five hundred miles of Memphis. He could even point out that Nance and Tisdale had testified about events occurring in other buildings while they were asleep in a different building. But Lester did not do that!

No, he just simply read off each charge against us and bored the jury to death. He didn't argue anything for us. He spent twenty minutes reviewing everything negative about the charges and case against us! In the middle of it, I looked at Paul and shook my head no and gave him the slash across the throat sign. I mouthed the words, "He's killing us. We are dead." I think I could have done a better job as a fifth grader. I couldn't imagine a worse closing argument. Where was the outstanding lawyer we had seen at trial? Was he throwing the whole thing? We truly wondered. He even forgot to pass the card around so the jury could read the things Tisdale had said about us in the card and the PS about Nance planning to "tell lies that would make us laugh." We weren't laughing. He didn't even mention the drug tests we had taken showing we were clean. For the first time, I thought we might get convicted!

June did no better. She stammered around. We did insist she show the jury the card from Tisdale. She somehow managed to get that right, at least.

Much to my surprise, the AUSA attorney got a second closing argument. That's right! He went first and he also got to go last. It was in this last closing argument that he claimed hundreds of thousands of blister packets had been found in the burn barrel. The testimony by the officer that found them was that there were hundreds. He also said there were hundreds of empty ether cans in the lab. The testimony from the fireman who testified as to their presence was that there were fifty or sixty empty cans. He stated as fact many other

things that had never come up in the trial, and there was no objecting to anything he said or chance to rebut it. We had just witnessed
a master at work—a master who knew how to use a system that was
already rigged for the government.

I realized how dreadful it really was to see "UNITED STATES
OF AMERICA v. JACK AND KARA PHILLIPS." I had just had
that power turned on me, on us. My confidence wavered for the
first time. I was ready for it to be over. Thank God it was, and court
was finally adjourned. I didn't even speak to Lester or June. I wanted
them out of my face and out of my life. I couldn't even bear to look
at them.

CHAPTER 33

QUIET BEFORE THE STORM

We drove to Paul and Jen's house. All we could think about and talk about were the closing arguments—or lack thereof. Everyone agreed Lester had thrown in the towel. This outstanding lawyer floundered and failed in this closing argument. His last appearance before the jury that would decide our fate had been horrible. Was it on purpose? Was it just incompetence? We couldn't be sure. We just felt like he had failed so miserably at such a crucial time. In the moment he should have shined the brightest, he was like a candle that had just gone out. June, well, June Riley was just June Riley. We hadn't expected much from her, and we hadn't gotten much. It was also appalling that the deck was stacked so favorably in the government's favor. How could the AUSA go first and last? Was that fair? No one could challenge anything he said in that final closing argument.

When we got to Paul's house, we discovered that Mom and Dad wanted to go home to Rector for the weekend. Of course, Paul and Jen agreed to take them. We decided we would stay in Memphis Friday night and then drive up early Saturday morning to Rector too. We went home and rehashed the final day in court. It was unanimous that our attorneys had failed miserably. We went to bed early and slept soundly. At least we didn't have to go back to court until Monday.

We spent Saturday morning driving to Rector and then visiting with Kara's family in the morning. We went to her mom's and visited with her, Mandy, and her brothers. She wanted to spend some time in the house where she grew up. We drove around that afternoon and went by the high school and the theater and drove out to the river. We wanted to look at all the places that had meant so much to us growing up.

Saturday night we were at Mom's house, in the comfort of the sanctuary with her and Dad. Paul and Jen were there, so we had a real family time. Sunday morning, I was sitting in the living room, visiting with Mother, and watching life pass by through the picture window. Then a stranger in a strange car we didn't recognize pulled into the driveway.

Mom said, "Jack, who's that?"

I said, "I don't know." I got off the couch and walked toward the door. About that time, a man I had known since childhood got out of the car. It was Taylor Finch. I had played Little League baseball with Taylor's older brother, John, but I hadn't seen Taylor in twenty-five years. I went out and met him in the driveway. We shook hands and exchanged pleasantries.

He said his dad had passed away and he was in the area for the funeral. He said he had heard that Kara and I were in some trouble with the feds. I said yes and caught him up on the trial and the circumstances of it all. Here came the interesting part. He informed me he was the owner/operator of a private airline company that operated out of Texas. They chartered the rich and famous. He had flown celebrities all over the world. He said, "Jack, I want you to know I have been in trouble before myself. If you are in trouble with the feds, you are in real trouble. They just never lose. In fact, you are probably going to lose and go to jail. I came by to tell you to get Kara and come with me. I will have you in South America by court time tomorrow in a country with no extradition deal with the United States. I will move you every three months. No one will find you, and you and Kara will live better than you have ever lived. Anytime you want to see your family, I will arrange it all. Get Kara, and let's move."

I was so surprised I couldn't say anything. Of course, eventually I refused. I told Taylor about my children and grandchildren and the failing health of Mom and Dad and Kara's mom. I just couldn't leave. Besides, I told him, "We are not going to lose. We are going to win. Taylor, we are innocent. We really are innocent, and they couldn't prove we had done anything wrong." He shook my hand, wished us luck, got in his car, and left. Three hours later, we were back home in Memphis.

I sat down that Sunday evening with all my bills, credit cards, and address book. I wrote down every relevant number, from driver's license to bank account and credit card numbers. I included addresses and even phone numbers if I had them. Everything important in our life that I could think of or find, I included in the record I made in the address book. I put the address book along with my billfold and watch inside my briefcase. I would leave the briefcase in Paul's car after I showed everything to him in case things did go bad tomorrow.

That night, Sunday, August 9, 1998, Kara and I went to bed and locked the door. We made love and held each other until the wee hours of the morning. We both realized if we lost, it might be a long time until we were intimate again. I don't think she and I had ever spent a night closer than we were that night. I don't know about Kara, but I never went to sleep at all.

On Monday morning, we were up early. Everyone seemed to be in a confident, joyous mood. We would win and this would all be behind us and we could move on with our life. Everyone at the house couldn't wait to get to Court to get the good news. We had even had some distant friends call Sunday night and say they would be there Monday to support us and celebrate with us.

We drove on over to Paul's early that day. Paul and Jen were both upbeat, like everyone at the house had been. I can't say we were upbeat. I couldn't describe our mood properly. I hugged and held on to Mom and Dad just a little longer than usual that morning before we went to court. It just seemed hard to let them go.

On the way in, I opened up my briefcase and began reviewing with Paul everything in there and in my address book. I showed him where I had listed the account numbers, addresses, and relevant phone numbers. I showed him my billfold and keys and the watch and sunglasses I was leaving in my briefcase. I told Paul if things went bad, everything he needed to handle our affairs was in that briefcase.

From the backseat, Jen said, "Jack, put that up. You're not going to need that! I've already made reservations for us tonight. We're going out to a fancy restaurant to celebrate. It's all on me."

Typical Jen. I looked back at her and said, "Jen, I hope you are right!"

When they let us out that Monday morning, I left my briefcase in the car. I had nothing in my pockets and didn't wear my watch. We knew our fate would soon be decided.

CHAPTER 34

TRIAL DAY 6: MONDAY, AUGUST 10, 1998 THE VERDICT

Court was called to order at 9:38 a.m. I didn't wear a suit, only a necktie and dress pants. Jury instructions were given by the judge. The jury began deliberating at 10:13 a.m.

As we entered the courtroom hallway that morning, it was clear there would be a crowd inside the courtroom. We must have had at least fifty supporters there to encourage us. The mood of everyone was upbeat. You couldn't have found one person in the entire group that believed we would be convicted. There were a lot of hugs, handshakes, smiles, and encouraging words.

Later, many of us went to lunch together. Around 1:30 p.m., the jury asked to see the video and hear the audiotapes again. They wanted to take another look and listen. Then, the jury asked the judge a question via a note. Deliberations began again around 3:00 p.m. At 3:27 p.m., the judge received a note from the jury. They were finally brought back into the courtroom at 4:57 p.m. to announce their verdict.

The courtroom became silent. We are asked to stand, and we did. The verdict was announced by the jury forewoman at 4:57 p.m.

For Jack Phillips, as to counts 1, 2, and 3—*guilty!* For Kara Phillips, as to counts 1 and 2—*Guilty!* The jury was polled. It was a unanimous verdict.

There was a huge gasp from the audience. The weeping began. There was almost a collective "No!" Mary Lynn, our beloved daughter, was perhaps the most affected. She was devastated. I couldn't move. I couldn't think. The unthinkable had happened to us.

Kara broke down. I had never seen her weep so hard. We were remanded to the custody of the US marshals until sentencing. There would be no bond or bail. I was told to remove my belt and necktie and empty my pockets. My pockets were already emptied, so I removed my tie and belt. They were passed over to Paul. Sentencing was set for November 13, 1998. Kara and I were going to jail. We were handcuffed right in the courtroom and led away. Our family and supporters were as stunned as we were. The trial was finally over. Court adjourned at 5:05 p.m.

They took us upstairs to the same little room where they had taken us back in February when we were waiting for Paul to bring the bail money. Unlike that time, this time we were handcuffed and the door was locked. Kara was sobbing. I didn't know what to say or how to comfort her. We hugged and cried and hugged and cried some more.

About twenty minutes later, the door was unlocked. They told Kara to step outside. She looked at me and said, "Good-bye, Jack." I said, "Good-bye, Kara. Stay strong. It's not over." She nodded, and they left. Another marshal told me to step out. I did. He undid the handcuffs and recuffed me in front. He picked up some leg shackles and attached them to my ankles. He then ran a chain from the ankle shackles to the handcuffs to complete the shackling process. I asked him, "Where am I going?" He said, "To Mason." I had been there before. I didn't know where Kara was going. I just knew I wouldn't see her again until sentencing, and that was three months away. I had not gone three months without seeing her since I was five years old. I just couldn't imagine not seeing her for three months.

Five days at Mason had seemed like an eternity. What would three months seem like? I had made arrangements the week before with the realtor for Ricky and Byron to stay in the house if this happened. At least it would be intact. I didn't know if Kara could do three months. In fact, I didn't know if I could.

CHAPTER 35

AFTER THE VERDICT: MONDAY, AUGUST 10, 1998

Kara was gone. I was taken downstairs to wait for the van that would take me to Mason. The attitude of the marshals were different. Now, I was a convicted felon and would be treated accordingly. I was in the basement of the federal building near a door that opened to the underground garage. I was fully shackled. They placed me in a chair in the hallway and ignored me. About 6:00 p.m., the van showed up. I recognized both of the guards from Mason.

They exchanged the marshals' shackles for their own shackles. The shackles from Mason included a large black box near the handcuffs. It was extremely uncomfortable and created a real hurt on the wrist bones of both hands. It seemed I would be the only passenger in the enclosed van. They took me around back, unlocked the doors with a key, and stuffed me in the back of the van. I grabbed a seat on the bench on the left side in the cargo area of the van. A thick metal cage separated the back of the van from the front, where the two guards sat. Both guards were black, and the radio was blaring WKNO, an all-black radio station in Memphis. The volume was cranked up loud.

We pulled out of the garage on Front Street and drove north, finally getting on the interstate bypass that would take us to Interstate

40 east toward Nashville and the Mason exit off I-40. It would take about forty-five minutes to reach the facility at Mason.

Finally, I was alone with my thoughts. People say when they think they are going to die, their whole life flashes before them. Although I wasn't facing death, I experienced my life flashing through my mind's eye. Mom and Dad; my children and grandchildren; Kara; Paul, Jen, and their son, Abel; my students; my track athletes; almost twenty years of teaching and coaching; my career; my friends; all those people that had been trying to help—it all flashed before my mind.

I had been a Christian since childhood. I had been raised in the church. I had taught Bible at my first teaching/coaching job in a private Christian school, but my personal life had fallen short of what it should have been. I couldn't help but ask now, "Why, God? Why me, God? Why now, God?" I wish I could tell you God spoke to me and gave me great insight or even an answer, but he didn't. At least not audibly.

I did have an answer that came to me in my mind and in my spirit. The answer that came was, "Why not you? What have I ever asked of you?" I don't know where specifically the thought or feeling came from, but I can say it was a profound thought and a profound moment in my life. Truthfully, God had never really asked anything of me. He had given me the desires of my heart: Kara, my childhood sweetheart; a precious daughter and son; a career coaching football with my brother, Paul, just has we had always hoped to do. We had even had an undefeated state championship team. I had played basketball and baseball in college and had been chosen All-State in basketball in Arkansas in high school, the first basketball player from my school to ever win such an honor. My picture shooting a basketball could still be found in the trophy case in the lobby of our high school gym. My 2-S draft deferment to attend college had even kept me safe and out of Vietnam. God had been so good to me.

I truly believed he was asking me now, "Will you honor me? When everything is taken away, will you find and keep your faith, or will you denounce me and lose your faith?" I determined in that short drive to Mason that I would serve him no matter what. I made a vow that I would leave prison better spiritually, emotionally, mentally, and physically than when I came in. I knew it would be a hard vow to keep. I wouldn't ask "Why me?" again. I wouldn't question God. I wouldn't blame God for my being where I was. I knew he could have stopped it, but I was also sure he didn't cause it. He just allowed it. I would trust and believe and keep my faith. This was the most poignant moment in my life since the fire. I felt a calming peace come over me.

The van exited the interstate and drove through the rural town that was Mason. There on Jimmy Naifeh Road set the Correctional Corporation of America's private prison, which would be my home for at least the next three months. It must have been about 7:15 p.m. when the van pulled up in front of the gate. The gate opened, and we drove through and stopped in front of the door that would take me inside the institution once again. This time, there would be no bail in five days. I was going to be here a little while.

CHAPTER 36

CHECKING IN AT MASON

As soon as we walked in the door, they removed the shackles. My wrists were sore, and my ankles were chafed from the ankle bracelets. I was taken down the hallway toward the office where the receiving cell was located. I was struck again by the lines on the floor in the hallway. There were the familiar red lines just a few feet away from the wall on both sides of the hallway. I was supposed to walk between the red line and the wall on the right side of the hallway. There was a yellow line right down the middle of the hallway. Everyone, guards included, was to walk to the right of the yellow line at all times.

They took me into the office and told the officer behind the desk who I was. He looked through a stack of papers on his desk and seemed to find one sheet that pertained to me. He motioned for the officers to put me in the holding cell in the back of the room. It was the same room I had been placed in on my arrival and departure back in February. This time, there were about fifteen inmates in blue jumpsuits that read MCSD on the back in large letters. These men were from the Madison County Sheriff's Department. They were from the Jackson, Tennessee, area. They would all be processed in before me. I was going to be here a while.

The private prison held prisoners on contract from Madison County Tennessee, the Virgin Islands, Hawaii, prisoners from West Tennessee, and federal inmates that would never be allowed to come into contact with any of the state, county, or territory inmates. Also, there were no violent offenders among the federal inmates. The federal inmates were all nonviolent and awaiting trial or going to trial or had been to trial and were awaiting sentencing. On the other hand, some of the state, county, and territory inmates were violent offenders. Some were even doing life sentences for murder. We would not be allowed to have contact with these 800 or so inmates. There were about 120 federal inmates. We couldn't work, go to the library, or go to medical or anywhere else unless all state/county/territory inmates were absent from those places and the hallway we would have to walk down to reach our destination. Even the Rec. yards were separated by a ten-foot-high chain-link fence. Occasionally, we would stand ten to fifteen feet away from the fence and talk to the other inmates while at Rec. We weren't supposed to, but the guards didn't enforce it as long as we weren't close enough to pass contraband through the fence.

They didn't get around to processing me until around 4:00 a.m. I was taken to laundry and given my prison clothes. That included three dark-red short-sleeved shirts and three pairs of matching pants with elastic waistbands. I received three pairs of white socks, three boxer shorts, and three T-shirts. I was also given three towels, three washcloths, and a package with samples of toothpaste, a small toothbrush, and soap and shampoo samples.

I was taken to A-Pod and placed in an end room by myself (A-101). The door (electronically controlled from the bubble control center) was slammed and automatically locked as I was placed in my cell. It was me, a commode, a sink, and a mirror along with a bunk bed with a one-inch mattress on each bunk. I had also been given a bedroll in laundry with a pillow, sheet, and blanket. I made up my bed and tried to sleep, but my mind would not slow down. I was worried about Kara.

I seemed frozen in time. I wanted to think about the future and what prison time would hold for me. I couldn't stop going back to the trial. I couldn't figure out how they found us guilty! I couldn't escape the lies, the false insinuations, and the complete misrepresentations. However, I kept finding myself at 711 Highway 72 in Bartlett, Tennessee. I was at my house, in my bed, driving my car, wearing my clothes, watching my TV, with my wife. That was just fantasy. It was rooted in reality, but it was not real and no longer even possible.

Besides, I learned later the ten cells upstairs in A-Pod held twenty men (two to a cell) who actually belonged in segregated housing (called the shu or the hole) for rules violations. One of these men was banging on his door with some object and screaming "Let me out! Let me out!" He never stopped. It was the loudest and most desperate wailing I had ever heard. He kept it up for hours. It never ended. At 6:00 a.m., he was still screaming at the top of his lungs and banging as loud as he could.

I wrote down my impressions of that night later. It was a clear example of just how inhumane men can be to one another. I didn't know what he had done, but it was clear to me he was like a caged animal. I thought he might be or might go insane. I couldn't listen to that night after night and not lose my own mind. What had I gotten myself into? Only time would tell.

CHAPTER 37

FIRST FULL DAY AT MASON

The electric door on my cell finally opened at 6:00 a.m. I hadn't slept at all. The only place I could go was out the door and in the dayroom, but I was ready to get out of the cell. The TV, about fifteen feet off the ground, was on full volume. The acoustics were so bad I couldn't make out a word, but it was roaring. Loudly. I stepped out the door, and just as I did, the inmate next door stepped out beside me. He said, "Good morning."

I replied, "Morning."

He kind of sized me up with his eyes and then said, "I know who you are. You're the schoolteacher on the meth case. You and your wife got convicted yesterday. Sam Nance testified against you."

I was shocked that he knew that. I said, "That's right. How do you know all of this?"

"I've been following your case. Descussio is my prosecutor too," he said, "and he's so corrupt he should be disbarred."

"How do you know about Nance?" I asked.

"He's here. He's been here about three weeks. We were at Rec., and he was out there bragging about setting up a teacher and his wife so he wouldn't be prosecuted. He was telling everybody if they were guilty, they needed to blame someone for a crime," he told me.

I asked him, "Would you write that down and be willing to testify about what all he said?"

'Yes," he said, "he was cheating keeping score in the volleyball game at Rec., and I asked him if he was the 5K1 of volleyball scorekeeping."

"What's 5K1?" I asked.

He told me, "That's telling on somebody to get a deal from the government."

"What did he say?" I asked.

"He reached under the volleyball net and grabbed me around the neck. A bunch of guys broke it up," he said.

"Will you write that down and give me the names of the other men that heard and saw it?" I asked.

"Sure," he said, "I can't stand that bastard."

I stuck out my hand and said, "Hi, I am Jack Phillips."

He took my hand and said, "I'm Keith Hawkins. Nice to meet you. Come on in my cell, and I'll write that stuff up for you."

I followed him into his cell. He pulled out a yellow legal pad and began to write. On one page, he listed the names of all the men in the volleyball game—he seemed to know them all—and even indicated which dorm or pod they lived in. He then wrote out a three-page account documenting Nance's boasting. He included the fact that Timmy Tisdale was also there. He told me which dorm they lived in. It was at the other end of the facility. Some of the men in the volleyball game lived in the same dorm they did. I asked Keith how I could talk to them. He told me we could talk to them at Rec. or at church or send messages to them through men from their dorm that did come to church.

He asked me who my lawyer was and when sentencing was scheduled. I told him, and then we were interrupted by breakfast. Breakfast, like all the other meals at Mason, would be served to us in the dayroom on trays. We never left the dayroom to go eat. Keith told me we would be allowed to go to Rec. after breakfast for one hour and then again after 4:00 p.m. count for one hour if we wanted to. I wanted to.

I spent the rest of that morning with my counselor. She set up some phone numbers for me to use to my brother's house, to Mom and Dad's house, to my daughter's house, to my son's house, and to my own house. I even added Kara's mom's phone number to my list. Those phone numbers were instantly approved since everyone was family. I also filled out visitation forms for all our family members. I was given rule sheets and a stack of papers and told to read them.

I had to go to medical for a preliminary exam that afternoon. It was always difficult to get permission to go down the hallway. The officer in the control booth had to make sure there were no state, county, or territorial inmates in the hallway or near where any federal inmate might be going.

As I returned to my unit after my visit with medical, I saw J-Dorm lined up to sign out and go to Rec. The second man in line was Sam Nance! That's how I knew it must be J-Dorm. He smiled at me and gave a little wave. I was overcome with emotion and found myself crossing the red line and yellow lines in the hallway. I was going after him. The officer saw me and stepped toward me and screamed, "Stop! Get back behind your line *now!*"

I hesitated. I knew I could whip that guard if I had to. I wanted to get to Sam Nance. The officer said something into his radio, and almost instantly, two guards came running around the corner. They shoved me over and back against the wall and said, "Assume the position!" I wasn't sure what that was, but I put my hands up on the wall. They told me to spread my feet. I did.

J-Dorm went on out to Rec. The guards patted me down and asked me what I was doing. I told them about Sam Nance. They seemed to understand. I told them I thought he was mocking me.

They relaxed and told me to go on down the hall and tell my counselor what had just happened. I did that.

I told her, "Don't put me in that position again. Keep Nance and Tisdale away from me or I might hurt them. I can't be responsible if you allow me to be put in that situation again! Do you understand?"

She nodded and said, "It won't happen again, Mr. Phillips. And I'm sorry."

Keith and I sat up most of the day talking about my case. He told me there was Rec. later that day and we would go outside for a while. He also said there would be a church service that night (as there was every Tuesday night at Mason) and we would send word to the men in A-Dorm on the list and try to get more written statements.

We ate lunch. I can't remember what we had, or maybe it was that I couldn't recognize what we had. Most of the afternoon was spent back in medical for more examinations.

After 4:00 p.m. count, I put on my dress shoes (they were the only shoes I had at this point), and Keith and I lined up in the hallway near a door. We had to sign out with our name and institution number they had assigned us on a sheet that said A-Pod Recreation at the top.

Keith and I went out to Rec. It really wasn't much, just a dirt track. There was an open pavilion too, and when I was here before, it had some free weights there. Keith told me a man had used one of the barbells to pry open one of the gates on the Rec. yard fence. There were double fences with double gates around the Rec. yard with razor wire on top. He had pried one gate open enough to crawl through. However, he left the barbell outside the first gate, so he couldn't get the second gate open enough to crawl out. He was caught between the two fences. As a result, the free weights were now gone.

Keith and I walked a lap on the track. He was telling me about his case. He was in for allegedly planning an armed robbery on a Brinks truck. He said the FBI used a paid informant to entrap him. He claimed Terry Descussio knew all about it and was the one person behind his prosecution. As we finished our lap, Keith said his back was bothering him, so he dropped out and said he'd wait under the pavilion. By the time we had signed out and walked a lap, we only had about twenty minutes left for Rec. Inmates from Montana were out on the other side of the fence on their Rec. yard. It was nicer than ours. It had a soccer field and a paved track.

As I started my second lap, I began to hear "Coach Phillips! Coach Phillips!" I stopped and turned around. This young man in his twenties came running down the track toward me. As he got near, he said, "Aren't you Coach Phillips that used to coach and teach at Hardeman County High School?"

I said, "Yes."

He said, "Coach, I was in the third grade with your daughter, Mary Lynn. You had my sister Trina in your class. You were her favorite teacher."

I asked him, "What's your name?"

He told me, "Brent Frazier."

I said, "Yeah, I did have your sister in class. Trina had blond curly hair and a chipped front tooth."

He smiled and said, "You really were her favorite teacher. She talked about you all the time."

"She smiled all the time and made really good grades. Your sister was a beautiful young lady and a really nice, polite person," I told him.

He smiled again and said, "Thanks, Coach. Coach, are you the Phillips that is in trouble over a meth lab in Memphis?"

I said, "Yeah, that would be me."

He said, "I heard all about it on TV and read it in the Memphis newspaper, but I had no idea it was you, Coach."

"It's me," I said, "and my wife too."

As we rounded the corner of the track and hit the straightaway, he pointed to a man with a beard leaning against the only tree on the Rec. yard. He said, "Do you know that guy, Coach?"

I said, "No, I don't think so." The man had long hair and a beard, but I was sure I had never seen him before. I asked Brent, "Why? Does he know me?"

Brent said, "I don't think so, Coach, but he's here on your case!"

I stopped walking and looked at both of them back and forth. "What could he know about my case? My case is over. He didn't testify," I said.

Brent said, "I don't know, Coach, but he's my cellie. He's been here three weeks."

I asked him, "What's that guy's name?"

He said, "Mike Fields."

By this time, we had walked past Mike Fields and were making good progress on another lap. I told Brent I was sure I did not know Mike Fields. About that time, the Rec. officer blew a whistle. That meant Rec. was over and we had to go back inside. Our time was up.

I told Brent to tell his cellie (Mike Fields) that I wanted to talk to him the next morning.

He said, "Okay, Coach, I'll tell him."

We shook hands and headed toward the doors at different ends of the facility that would take us back to our units. As Keith and I went in, I told him about Brent and the man, Mike Fields. Keith told me they were both in the same dorm as Nance and Tisdale. Now I really was curious.

That night, I heard all of Keith's story. It was as tragic as my mine. We had much in common. He was a ship's captain and had steered luxury vacation cruise ships all over the world. His title was Captain Hawkins. His dad was a retired military man. He had been an officer on the ship involved in the Gulf of Tonkin incident. That incident had resulted in a Congressional resolution that launched our country into the Vietnam War, in a legal sense.

I was anxious to see Mike Fields again. I was also exhausted. I was glad I didn't have a roommate (cellie). I went to bed early but was up and awake when the door popped open at 6:00 a.m.

MIKE FIELDS

had breakfast while watching cartoons on TV. There was a twenty-something black man that seemed to control the TV from 6:00–8:00 a.m. He turned to the cartoons and sat in front of the TV, staring up. I was eager for Rec. call.

At about six forty, they made the call. I was ready. I was the first one out the door and down the hallway. I waited by the door to the Rec. yard. Finally, the officer with the clipboard showed up, and I signed and went out the door.

Our pod was the first one out that morning. I rushed over to the door where the men from J-Dorm would come through. About five minutes passed before the door was opened and the men began pouring out. Brent Frazier, the kid I knew, was about the ninth man out. I grabbed him by the arm and asked him, "Where's your cellie? Where's Mike Fields?"

He said, "Coach, you're not going to believe this, but they came and got him about 2:00 a.m. to take him back to prison in Marion (Illinois)."

"Did you ask him what he knew about my case?" I asked.

"No," he said," I just told him you wanted to talk to him."

I couldn't believe Mike Fields had slipped through my fingers. I said, "You never asked him or heard him say anything about my case?"

"Nope," he replied.

I said, "What about Nance and Tisdale? Are they still here?"

"No," he said, "they took them out too."

I asked Brent, "Did you ever hear Nance and Tisdale talking about why they were here?"

"Yeah," he said, "I did."

"What did they say?" I asked.

"Well, at first they were telling everybody they were here because the feds were trying to give them another case. But when Mike got here, they changed their tune. They said they were testifying against a man and woman so they wouldn't catch another charge."

"That's exactly what they said?" I asked.

"Yes," he replied.

I asked Brent if he would be willing to write that down and sign it. He said he would. I found out that he was in prison for having marijuana sent to his house via UPS. He said he was going to plead guilty and try to reduce his time. He said they had him dead to rights.

I was disappointed. I was still in evidence-gathering mode, I guess. I wanted to know what Mike Fields knew about my case. The fact he had not testified just intrigued me more. Nance and Tisdale never mentioned him either. Now he was gone, and it seemed improbable that I would ever see him or get that information. They closed the Rec. yard. I said good-bye to Brent and thanked him for trying to help. I told him to send his written statement to me through one of the men coming to church that night (or bring it himself if he was coming). He said he would do that. I wouldn't see Brent Frazier again for eleven months.

CHAPTER 39

TELEPHONES

I learned how to use the phones that morning. I called my mom and dad. Later that afternoon, after school, I called Paul and told him I needed some money on my account. I also told him I owed three hundred dollars to the court for an assessment fee, and Kara owed two hundred dollars. There was a one-hundred-dollar charge for each count we were convicted on. Paul said he would bring some money over to the institution immediately and take care of the court costs the next day. I needed the money on my account for commissary. Paul said he had not heard from Kara and wasn't even sure where she was.

The telephones at Mason were set into a concrete kiosk that included a built in place to sit. There were places for four phones and seats, but only three of the phones actually worked. A prisoner could only talk for fifteen minutes at a time. Then we had to wait at least thirty minutes to use the phones again. At this point, there were only nineteen inmates in A-Pod because the twenty men upstairs were all in segregated housing. They could only use the phone once a day, one man at a time, after we were locked in our rooms. It wasn't too hard to get to a phone. Another drawback to using the phones was the cost. Each call had to be collect, even local calls, so if you talked fifteen minutes, it cost $7.50 per call.

Paul did make it over before 5:00 p.m. and put one hundred dollars on my account. In reading through the material the counselor had given me, I discovered I could order sweats, shorts, tennis shoes, gloves, and sock hats from either JCPenney or from Eastbay, a catalog company. I made a list of what I wanted and needed.

That afternoon after 5:00 p.m., I called my house and talked to Ricky Short. He and Byron were doing fine and living there together. They assured me everything at home was still intact. That was encouraging.

Later that night, I called Paul and Jen again. They had heard from Kara. She was still at 201 Poplar but would be moving by the end of the week. She didn't know where she would be going. Paul said he and Jen were both worried about Kara and me. He asked me how I was doing. I knew Kara and I couldn't write directly to each other from jail to jail, but I told Paul I would write Kara and send the letter to him, and he could mail it to her when she got settled with an address. She could write me and send it to him, and he could mail her letters to me too. He said he would take care of that and explain it to Kara. I gave him my mailing address and institution number.

I also gave him a list of the things I wanted from JCPenney. He said he would have Jen get that for me and have it sent to me. I reminded him that the store had to mail it directly to me. He couldn't buy it and mail it to me himself. It had to come from the store.

Keith was a real help in those early days. He led me through many details of how to be locked up there and get along. I learned about the set count times when all the inmates had to return to their cells, shut the doors, and wait to be counted. It was a big deal. The officers came by to count and make sure everyone was there. Lunch was served shortly after the 10:00 a.m. count and dinner shortly after the 4:00 p.m. count. We did have a microwave oven in the unit. It was in use almost continually all day long. Men cooked food in plastic bowls they purchased in commissary.

The commissary was simply a store. There was a commissary list that had all the items for sale and their prices. They sold food, soft drinks, paper, and pens. An inmate could buy envelopes for mailing letters that were prestamped with postage. We could not buy stamps. The cost of postage was included in the price for each individual envelope purchased. We could also get copies made there for ten cents per page per copy. They sold name-brand cigarettes and matchbooks that cost a penny a piece. Most of the men smoked. My store day would be on Thursday each week. It was determined by a portion of your assigned institutional number. I was allowed to spend fifty dollars per week at the store. The prices of everything were all jacked up. With the poor quality of the meals, the commissary became indispensable. Going to the commissary was often the highlight of the week.

Even though federal inmates couldn't work there, they were part of an elaborate theft ring. The kitchen workers were Virgin Island inmates, and the Montana inmates pushed the food carts from pod to pod or unit to unit. They also brought in Igloo coolers that contained either Kool-Aid or tea. A second Igloo cooler contained nothing but ice (supposedly). At every meal, vegetables, meat, cheese, or other eatable items were smuggled in under the ice in the ice cooler. If you watched carefully, you would see the signals passed with just a nod or look. I wasn't sure how the payment for the items worked, but I am sure everything was ultimately paid for.

There were also inmates there smoking pot every day. We could almost always smell it in the unit. It had to have been smuggled in by the guards (or so I thought). I know some of the guards did bring in pot, but it was also introduced into the institution by being thrown over the fence at the Rec. yard at night. There was a paved road that passed just on the east side of the Rec. yard not more than twenty feet from the fence. Late at night, people just drove down the road and throw the contraband over the fence in a bag or even a McDonald's sack. Inmates picked it up when they went to Rec. in the morning. We were often patted down as we came in from the Rec. yard, but that wasn't always the case. Even when we were, it was half-hearted by the guards. These officers were minimum-wage employees. The institution got what they paid for in quality—really not too much!

From time to time, they conducted shakedowns. They often found drugs or other contraband. They sent the men to the hole, so men were constantly going to and coming from the shu. I was really just getting my feet wet in regard to prison living. Keith helped a lot. I couldn't believe all the games and the hustling that was going on. Everyone seemed to be working and looking out just for themselves and working every conceivable angle.

CHAPTER 40

TIME MOVING ON

Men continued to come and go back and forth to court. Some were going for hearings, some for trial, and others for sentencing. Men were transferred regularly to the Bureau of Prison facilities to begin serving their sentences after their sentence hearings. New men showed up daily. It was like a revolving door there.

There were changes at the Mason facility too, even that first week. The contract with North Carolina expired, and all the North Carolina inmates left. The men upstairs in my pod were removed and taken to segregated housing, where they were supposed to be. A-Pod was then filled with more federal inmates, like me, and the other eighteen that had been there. We went from nineteen inmates to forty inmates overnight. I had a new cellmate (cellie). His name was James. He had been shot in the abdomen, and the bullet had exited his back. It had done extensive damage, and he had just been released from the hospital. There was a real problem: James had a colostomy bag. The facility didn't have the proper size bag to match his equipment. If he used what they gave him, it leaked and really stunk up the cell. If he didn't use it, he had to wash out the old one and reuse it. I've never smelled anything so foul in my life. It was nasty. I know it wasn't James's fault, but I kept finding myself getting mad at him. He was the one truly suffering. My suffering was secondary to his.

Using the telephone became a real difficult issue. A prisoner had to stand in line and wait and wait and wait. There was always someone who thought he was too good to wait in line like everyone else. He would tell the man behind him "Save my spot." That created all kinds of problems.

Also, we now had forty men eating each meal. There were long lines for the food trays and for the ice and tea or Kool-Aid. This ice cooler at mealtime was the only opportunity to get ice. We had sodas, but we didn't get ice except in the Igloo coolers at mealtime. Some guards brought in a cooler of ice about eight thirty at night too. Ice was scarce. The ice cooler always produced a mad scramble. Men were also bad about sticking their own cup down in the ice and scoping up a cup for themselves. There was a clean cup inside the cooler men were supposed to use so they wouldn't contaminate the ice for everyone else. Not everyone used this provided cup. I am sure all kinds of germs were passed in the ice.

I continued to go to Rec. at each and every opportunity to at least walk. I spent all my free time with Keith. We both continued to share the intricacies of our cases with each other. We both claimed to be innocent. We both felt like Terry Descussio, the AUSA, was total corruption. We both felt we had been deprived of even a hint of a fair trial and justice. He had lost a career and had gone almost two years without seeing his two little boys. He had spent almost half a million dollars on attorneys and discovered, like I had, they really didn't care much and didn't even try.

Keith spread the word about my needing written statements concerning Nance and Tisdale. I got Brent's statement, so I already had Keith's and Brent's. I picked up three or four more from men in my unit. I felt good about the letters. They seemed to be evidence we had been set up by Nance and Tisdale. I decided I would take them to sentencing with me. I still had some fight left. When I went to the store, I got copies of everything. If it was legal work, an inmate could often get copies made even if it wasn't your store day. I always made and sent copies to Lester Moore, June Riley, Paul, and Kara. I also kept a copy for myself. Paul made copies and passed them to Phillip (Phil) Watson. Phil was an attorney in Memphis. Phil had played football on one of our teams and gone to college on a football scholarship. Later, he went to law school. He had been practicing law about a dozen years. Phil agreed to help Paul as he tried to dig up more evidence on our case. Phil was a huge help. As soon as I received a copy of the trial transcript, I made a copy of that for Paul and Phil too.

I continued calling Mom and Dad every day. Dad really wasn't talking very much, but we would talk from time to time. I could tell his health was failing. Mom was always upbeat. I also called Paul every day. He told me Jen had purchased everything I wanted from JCPenney. He also said he was coming to visit me on Saturday. He had called and gotten the information and found he was approved to visit. He knew more about visitation than I did.

Friday night, I found out Kara had been moved to the Hardeman County Jail. It was a brand-new facility and met federal standards. It was ironic she was incarcerated in the rural West Tennessee county where we had lived and I had taught school and coached. Paul said he had mailed the letter to her I had written. He said Kara would be sending me a letter soon.

The visit Saturday morning was the real highlight of my first week. Paul and Jen both showed up. I had to pass through a small room about the size of a walk-in closet. They took two of us inmates going to visitation into this little room at the same time. A prisoner could not go into visitation without passing through this room. Once inside, they told us both to strip naked. We both did. We piled our prison clothes on the floor. The officer picked up each piece of our clothing and shook it out. He told us to open our mouths so he could look inside. We had to run our hands through our hair and let him look in our ears. We were told to lift our nut sacks so he could look underneath there. Finally, we were told to squat and cough. Some officers had you turn around and spread your butt cheeks and squat and cough. This process was repeated every time we came out of visitation also.

Paul told me at the visit he had been trying to talk to Lester Moore about the statements we had been collecting. We also discussed a special plan for calling home. Radio Shack had a device that could handle two different phones. Paul had two different lines and two different numbers. If I called one number and Kara called the other number at the same time, he could lay the phones in the device, and we could have a conversation. There were a few problems. The device just amplified our voices into the room. Everyone could hear us. There would be no privacy. Secondly, we couldn't both talk at the same time. Only one could speak at a time. The other had to listen and wait until the first person finished. Three-way calls were illegal. This was not illegal. Paul said he would purchase the device that afternoon and set it up when we called him that night. It should be in play on Sunday night.

I knew trying to call at a set time would be difficult if not impossible with forty men using three phones. How could I ensure a time? It would be really hard to do. All afternoon I watched the phones, and I noticed a large black man everyone called Cockroach overseeing the phones. He was at least keeping order. He had been in prison before and was involved in most of the illegal activities in our pod, but he was doing a nice job of keeping order around the phones. I told him about my situation.

He said, "Coach, you just be here before 6:00 p.m. each night, and I will make sure you have a phone at six o'clock."

I had my doubts about whether he could really do that, but he made the guarantee. Surprisingly, I never missed a 6:00 p.m. call the entire time I was at Mason. It wasn't just Cockroach. All the men in the unit were willing to cooperate with me so I could talk to Kara (my wife) each night at six o'clock. We had little in common, but need was a commonality we all had and shared. No one ever complained, at least not to me, about letting me go ahead of them in line to make my call on time.

Monday night rolled around, and at 6:00 p.m. I called home. Paul said he was waiting for Kara to call on the other phone line. We didn't have to wait long. I heard the other phone rang, and Paul said, "Hang on just a minute, Jack." I heard him answer the phone with Kara, and then he said, "Go ahead, talk." Although we couldn't talk at the same instant, we could have a conversation. We learned how to be patient and wait for the other person to finish.

It was so good to hear her voice. She sounded good. She said the county jail was clean and the food was good. She said it was much better than 201 Poplar. She cried a little (and I might have too), but she assured me she would make it. She was looking forward to seeing me at sentencing as I was looking forward to seeing her. We both promised to write often. Those phone calls and letters became our mental and emotional salvation and helped us endure the separation a little bit better, especially in the early weeks and months.

We had written letters back and forth when I was in college and she was still in high school. We wrote each other a couple of times a week then. I came home every weekend to work at the local radio station, so we really weren't apart but a few nights a week.

Each day a prison guard came into the unit and shouted "Mail call!" Everyone gathered around. Most men didn't get any mail. It was a thrill to have your name called and receive a letter. If a prisoner did get a letter or letters, he rushed back to his cell to read his mail as fast as he could. We were starved for information from home. Then, he would read it again, more slowly this time. I kept every letter and often went back and read it for a third and even fourth time. I also decided to save every letter, so each month I packaged them in a large envelope, write the date on the envelope, and send them home. Paul put the big envelopes in my filing cabinet. I don't know why I did that. I just couldn't throw them away. A letter from Kara meant more than anything. Although all our mail was opened and read by some officer before we received it, it still had a feeling of privacy and intimacy about it. I made a vow that I would write Kara every day seven days a week. I could not stand the thought of her going to mail call and not having her name called. I fulfilled that vow. I wrote her a letter every day.

KEITH

The week of August 24, Keith's cellmate left, and I asked to move in with him. Permission was granted, and my life changed for the better. We became as close as brothers. He had gone to trial in May. I had gone to trial in August. We both had been found guilty and were awaiting sentencing. Most of the men in at Mason had plead "Guilty" and not gone to trial like we had. They would say, "You can't beat the feds, so just plead guilty for a lesser sentence." Keith and I had refused to plead guilty to something we didn't do, reduced sentence or not.

One of the common things we shared was that we both had tapes in our cases that had been altered. He talked our counselor into letting us use a cassette tape player to listen to his tapes. He also had the transcripts. It was really strange to see the tapes and transcripts didn't match up. Actually, he had been given two sets of tapes of the same conversation. Both tapes, it was claimed, were originals. However, they didn't even match each other. How could the tapes be true and accurate when they didn't match each other or the transcripts?

Keith stayed busy working on what he called a timeline. He said the timeline could prove the alleged events could not have happened in the required time frame. Keith showed me the alleged plans for the armed robbery and the times he was supposed to have been involved in its planning. The city, street, and address he had supposedly added didn't even exist anywhere! He made them up. Keith had purchased his own tape recorder to record the events himself. He was trying to get the real criminals on tape. His mom sent him the sales receipt for the tape recorder, and she had the empty box that she had taken from his truck after his arrest. The government denied they took his tape recorder, although they clearly did. That tape recorder was important. It would contain an unaltered tape that would show he had no part in the conspiracy. His mom had hired a tape man from Mississippi to look into the government tapes and decide if they were altered or not. That cost them five thousand dollars.

I was anxious to get my transcripts. Keith told me they would be altered. I had been told it would take six to eight weeks. Because I was indigent, I was not going to have to pay for my transcripts. About all I could do at this point was to go through the discovery materials Paul had sent me and look for discrepancies. I also made notes the best I could about certain testimonis I knew to be false. This would be a continuing an ongoing process.

On August 31, a Monday, a call came in over the intercom for me to report to laundry. I went there and had two packages. One was from Paul. It contained three books he had put together for me with plastic combs. They were years one, two, and three of a three-year Bible study course. I had him copy these from material I had used when teaching Bible at school.

Much to my surprise, the officer in charge asked if he could keep the Bible studies for a few days. He was a pastor and wanted to copy them and use them in his church. The request was really unusual. I would never have expected that. We had a nice talk about our Christian faith. He would keep and copy more Christian materials that came in for me.

The other package was from JCPenney. It contained the sweats, tennis shoes, and everything else Jen had ordered for me. The officer went through each piece. When he came to the sweatshirt, he frowned. I asked him if there was a problem. He said, "Yeah. You're not supposed to have a sweatshirt with a hood on it."

I told him no one had explained that to me. I asked him, "Should I just ship it back and have her exchange it?"

He thought a moment and said, "No, Mr. Phillips, I think that'll be all right this time." He smiled and handed me the sweatshirt. I knew I wouldn't be cold when winter came like I was in February after my arrest.

Over the course of weeks, I would have many conversations with the officer in laundry. He took almost every piece of my Christian mail home and copied it for use in his church. I had met a good Christian brother. He was black. I was white. He was an officer. I was an inmate. However, we had our faith in common.

C H A P T E R   4 2

MOVING

Later that fall, the first week of September, we had a big upheaval. Officers showed up and told us we were all moving. Some would go to B-Pod and others to one of the dorms. The move would occur over the next three days. In effect, they were emptying A-Pod. We weren't told why. Keith and I were very worried. We had grown comfortable with each other and didn't want to be separated. However, my name was the first one called. I was told to pack my things and go to B-Pod. Keith was told he would be moving in the next day or two. We begged and pleaded, but that was that.

I packed everything up in my laundry bags and went to B-Pod, right next door. They put me in a cell with a Hispanic guy named Roberto Gonzalez. He introduced himself to me as Nacho. He was really a friendly, gentle person, about forty years old. He had come to America when he was only six weeks old. All his family—mom, dad, brothers, sisters—lived in Kansas and were naturalized citizens. He lived in North Carolina. He had a wife and three children. His wife was also a naturalized citizen, so his children were citizens too. It was summer and just a few weeks before harvest (he worked on a farm in North Carolina), so he decided to take his wife and children and go visit his family in Kansas. He had talked to his sister, and he told her he had decided to fill out his naturalization papers while he was there. He said he should have done it twenty years ago but he had just neglected to do it. He was working hard, then got married, then had the children, and life just got busier and busier for him. He was a foreman on a large farm in North Carolina.

When he was passing through Memphis on his way to Kansas, the Drug Interdiction Squad pulled him over. They told him he was going sixty-five miles per hour in a fifty-five-miles-per-hour zone. He said he was only doing fifty-five miles per hour because he, like every other Hispanic that traveled through Memphis, knew they were apt to be stopped by law enforcement officials. There were other Hispanics at Mason that had suffered the same fate. Some were from Texas, others from Florida, and some from New York. All the Hispanics knew of the reputation of officers in Memphis. They all knew and expected to be stopped on some bogus traffic stop, have their car searched after being pulled over for drugs or cash (or both), be made to show their documentation, and then arrested if they didn't meet the criteria. Nacho had just driven into something larger than him. He was facing extradition to Mexico. That was a place he hadn't seen since he was six weeks old! He had no family or friends there. He said he guessed his wife and kids would move to Mexico and wait for him to be extradited to Mexico. His wife did have relatives there. He was really worried about living in Mexico and said it would be a cultural shock.

I found out the first night why they called him Nacho. He cooked either sixty-four or seventy-two burritos every night. If he made them, he made eighteen to twenty-four bowls. They paid him to cook their food by giving him his food free. He always got a portion of what he cooked.

I continued to see and meet with Keith at Rec. each day. I found out from the Montana boys that all six hundred or so of them were supposed to leave and go to a newly built state prison in Montana just any day.

We had some happy and carefree days during September and the early fall. There wasn't any pressure on us, at least not like the pressure we had before trial. We continued to work on our cases and accumulate what evidence we could. We often found the old saying "Two heads are better than one" to be true. We were simply a huge help to each other.

One of the interesting new items that fall of 1998 was the Bill Clinton–Monica Lewinsky fiasco. Keith and I often sat at a table while he wrote one-liner after one-liner about the situation. We laughed so hard. Many times I had to go to my cell, close the door, and lie down. Keith sent letters to David Letterman and Jay Leno. I actually heard several of those very jokes in the monologue over the next three years. They were brilliant and very funny.

Keith also made up a job application for workers at the institution. It was bogus, of course. By cutting and pasting real memos, he even had it on what appeared to be a letterhead. It was harmless fun but struck all the inmates as hilarious. Laughter was the medicine we all needed; Keith provided much of that for us.

CHAPTER 43

TUESDAY NIGHTS

The first Tuesday night I was at Mason (August 11, 1998), I went to church. It was held in a small classroom. It had plastic chairs set in rows of four on each side with a middle aisle between. I guess it was three or four rows deep. Up front, there was a podium and three more plastic chairs facing the audience.

I hadn't been at the facility much more than twenty-four hours, but I sensed a completely different feeling in that room. There wasn't any gloom and despair that seemed to cloud and cover every other aspect of inmate life there. All the inmates—black, white, and Hispanic—mixed freely. There were a lot of handshakes, hugs, and smiles. There was a warmth in that group completely lacking in our units. In the units, everyone and everything was separated by race. There were also gang affiliations and cliques. Those groups simply did not intermingle.

A black inmate was the emcee for the service. His name was Romy, and he was very upbeat and positive. His enthusiasm was infectious. Another inmate named Alfred gave his testimony and words of encouragement. He had great natural leadership qualities. A person could just tell. Romy led us in some praise songs, and then he called up another inmate named Michael to sing a special. He sang "As a Deer Panteth by the Water." I had only heard that song a few times. I am not even sure he got all the words right, but I had never heard the song sung without music in such a simple, childlike, compassionate way. It was sung with such feeling, and it was truly beautiful. When he finished, I had tears rolling down my face.

I was sitting on the aisle in the third row on the right side of the room. I had perfect view to the podium. It was a heartfelt service. For the first time, I personally sensed the commonality between us. We were inmates. We were caught up in something together. We were being swept away as if a storm was passing over us. All that gave us something special to share. We were actually sharing our fears, hopes, desires, and sufferings. I didn't feel so alone.

The guests were two older white men from the outside. They were from Bartlett, Tennessee. Brother Doug was the pastor of an independent church. I had driven by that church many times. His friend, Gil, was a funeral home director and a member of his church. They were both in their sixties. It was obvious to me they had been coming here for a while. They joked and conversed with the other men like old friends. There was a real easiness about the relationship.

Brother Doug let Gil say a few words, then he preached the sermon. He was so excited! He told a few jokes and had us laughing loudly. Then, he preached a great sermon. His joy bubbled over. It too was infectious. He lit up the room, and we all felt instantly better. I only recognized about half of the men in the room because the other half were from the dorms. I met some new men that night.

As Brother Doug finished up his sermon, he gave a rather traditional invitation and call for anyone to accept Jesus Christ as Lord and Savior. There were a few men that responded. Others rededicated their lives to the Lord and asked God to forgive them. It was almost comical to watch Brother Doug. He was so humble. He cried and wept as easily as he laughed. He truly wore his emotions on his sleeve. He was real in every sense of the word.

He asked Brother Gil to dismiss us with prayer. I stood up to leave and picked up the Bible I had brought with me. I had found it on top of the mailbox nailed to the wall. The Bible was actually in two pieces and had no cover. However, it was all there, but it wasn't too impressive looking.

As I shook hands with some of the men around me and said good-bye, I began making my way up the aisle toward the door. I saw Brother Doug laughing, shaking hands, and hugging some of the men, but he also seemed to be glancing my way from time to time. Eventually, he broke free and came right toward me. He was working his way back toward me, and I was working my way forward toward him and the door.

As we met, he stuck out his hand, and we shook. We exchanged our names, and he put his arm around my neck, leaned forward, and said into my ear, "Look, I don't know why you're here or anything about you, but the Holy Spirit has put it on my heart to tell you this: Don't worry about how much time you have to do. God's in control. You won't do however much time they give you. One day, your papers will pass over the warden's desk to release you. He won't even know where the papers came from, so don't worry. Okay?"

I was stunned. I wasn't just shocked by what he said. No. I was shocked because I *knew* he was speaking the truth. It was a supernatural knowledge from my heart, not my head. I had already had a really good spiritual experience at the church service. This took things to a different level. No one else ever heard what he said to me. I shook my head and said, "All right, thank you!" He just turned and walked away.

Brother Doug and Gil came back every Tuesday after that. Those services really encouraged me and served as an anchor. It made my transition so much easier and awakened my spiritual life. I had promised God. Now, God was equipping me for the long haul to fulfill my vow. That was what had spurred me to ask Paul to send the Bible studies. I was ready to teach the Bible studies. When I received them a few weeks later, I started teaching them in my cell each night. We averaged six to ten men. We read scripture, shared, and prayed. We helped one another. We gave value to time that would have otherwise been wasted.

C H A P T E R   4 4

NEW INMATES AND VIOLENCE

The Montana men were gone. The North Carolina men were gone. That meant we had empty spaces at Mason. The next group to come was the prisoners from Hawaii. Much of the violence and problems at the institution were caused by the inmates from Hawaii and the Virgin Islands. They just couldn't get along with their own people. They were constantly fighting among themselves. There was trouble from one or both of these groups almost daily.

They brought in another group of thirty or so inmates too. These were a special group. They were violent offenders from Washington, DC. The prison officials had spent over a month and a lot of money preparing A-Pod (my old unit) by reinforcing the doors with metal cages and installing metal cages over the shower stalls.

Many of the tables had been removed from the dayroom, and a large wooden table with two office chairs was placed in front of the room. There were supposed to be two officers in that unit at all times 24-7. Most of the time, we didn't even have one officer in our pod. Occasionally, the on-duty officer would walk through. Of course, they were present for all official counts too. The officers were equally men and women. When they did come in, it was often because they were simply bored.

In the A-Pod with the DC inmates, there was *always* to be two guards. Even then, only one inmate at a time was to ever be out of his cell. Never more than one! The inmate that was out was supposed to be handcuffed before his cell door was ever opened. The inmate would back up to the door (inside the cell) and place his hands behind his back and stick them out through the metal door and metal cage. He was handcuffed and then would step away from the door, and only then would his door be opened. These inmates were allowed one phone call per day. They were allowed a five-minute shower once a day. They would enter the shower stall fully handcuffed. They would back up to the door on the metal cage and stick their handcuffed hands through the slot. Their hands would be free for them to shower. When finished, they would do the process in reverse and get handcuffed again. They never left the shower stall / metal cage without being handcuffed securely. Because A-Pod and B-Pod shared a common sally port, we had a bird's-eye view of the security procedures in A-Pod.

When an inmate was in an open area (always handcuffed), one officer would get behind him and grab the handcuffs and lift his arms up in an awkward position. The other officer would then walk in front of the inmate. If he was making a phone call, his hands would be cuffed in front instead of behind his back so he could dial the phone.

It was the most control I had ever witnessed exercised on any inmate. Over a week or two, we got the whole view. We begin to notice the officers relaxing in their duties in A-Pod. About half the time, there was only one officer in the unit, not the required two. Some of the other officers talked openly about it. They said the facility was understaffed and didn't have enough officers to keep two in there 24-7. Some said they would not work in that unit by themselves because it was too dangerous to work in that unit alone.

We went to church one Tuesday night as usual, and when it was over, I raced back to the unit to use the bathroom. I went through the sally port alone because I was way ahead of the other men. I looked into A-Pod and saw a DC inmate talking on the phone at the kiosk. An officer we called Cockeye was working the unit alone. Ms. Brady was in the control bubble, and she popped the door for me to enter B-Pod almost immediately.

I ran to the cell, threw my Bible on the bed, and used the bathroom. I came out expecting to see Keith and the other men pouring into the unit. But there was no one coming in and no one in the sally port. I started walking back toward the sally port. As I got near, I could see Keith and the other men from B-Pod about twenty feet down the hallway stopped and all huddled together. I reasoned that an officer must have stopped them for some reason.

As I reached the sally port inside my unit, I saw a white man about thirty-five in an orange jumpsuit on his knees in the sally port. I knew he was a DC inmate because of the orange jumpsuit. He was a nice-looking man. He looked like a big strong guy, and his hands were on his stomach. Blood was oozing between his fingers and dripping and pooling on the sally port floor between his knees. He wasn't but about six feet from me as I looked through the window on my door. He looked up at me, and I mouthed the words "Are you all right?" He shook his head no and then mouthed "No."

About that time, Officer Applewhite (Cockeye) came in the sally port from the hallway. Had he been a white man, he would have been pale as a ghost. In fact, he was a black man that was literally pale as ghost. He walked over to the bleeding man, placed his hand on his shoulder, and said something to him.

The white man on his knees nodded then moved his hand on his bleeding stomach and grabbed the end of a black object protruding from his stomach. He pulled out a ten-inch to twelve-inch piece of metal that had been scraped and sharpened on one end. He handed the piece of metal to Cockeye. Cockeye stood there holding the bloody piece of metal as blood dripped on the floor, forming a new puddle. I looked at the piece of metal carefully. It was a piece of metal from a metal locker door. The piece that was just on the inside of the door running from top to bottom on any standard metal locker. I just stood there and watched the blood drip, drip, drip.

The man continued sitting on his knees on the sally port floor. It looked like he was trying to hold the blood in as it now seemed to pour between his fingers. In a matter of minutes, an acting lieutenant came in the sally port. He held the hallway door from the sally port open, and Cockeye helped the injured man out into the hallway. The door was wedged open, so I had a good view of him. He continued to bleed a lot.

I watched in horror as Cockeye raised the man's head and stuck a towel or coat or something under his head. I beat on the window of the door and screamed, "Don't elevate his head! Not his head! Raise his feet! Elevate his feet!" Over and over I yelled and beat on the glass. They looked at me but didn't seem to understand what I was saying.

Finally, a female medical officer arrived. She had both hands just full of gauze. I couldn't believe what she did! I guess I expected her to apply pressure to the wound to try to stem the flow of blood. She didn't do that. Instead of applying pressure, she stood over the man and just dropped both handfuls of gauze on his stomach. He tried to gather it up himself and press down on the wound, but he seemed to be fading and losing strength fast. He had lost an extraordinary amount of blood already. The hallway now had a larger pool of blood than either of the pools in the sally port.

The last straw came when another officer came down the hallway with a wheelchair (not a stretcher). I couldn't believe it! He needed a stretcher. He needed to elevate his feet. They actually lifted him up and *sat* him in the wheelchair. They took off toward medical with him sitting straight up. I had been watching for six to eight minutes.

After they were gone, they let Keith and the other inmates move in the hallway. Keith and a group came in B-Pod. I watched those men zigzag around all the blood in the hallway and the sally port.

Keith then related to me what he had seen from the hallway while I was in my cell using the bathroom. He and two or three other inmates had actually made it to the hallway sally port door. They had a perfect view into A-Pod. They saw the stabbed man sitting and talking on the phone. He was handcuffed in front. Cockeye was the only officer in the unit. Keith said Cockeye was standing and facing the man on the phone when a second inmate stepped out of a cell two doors from the end on the bottom range. He was not handcuffed. Keith said he had seen the piece of black metal in that inmate's hand. Neither Cockeye nor the inmate on the phone saw him coming. He ran around Cockeye and ran up to the man on the phone and stabbed, stabbed, stabbed, and stabbed until he lost his grip on the bloody, slippery piece of metal. It was left in the man's stomach. He had tried to rise, Keith said, but the man simply over-powered him.

When Cockeye saw what was happening, Keith said he ran toward the sally port door. Ms. Brady popped the door to the sally port and motioned for Keith and the men to move back down the hall toward the church classroom. She then popped the sally port door, and Cockeye entered the sally port and then on out into the hallway.

Cockeye got on his radio and began talking, Keith said. He only went back into A-Pod after the attacker had returned to his cell and slammed his door shut. He went into A-Pod and helped the victim into the sally port. He put him on his knees in the position he was in when I came to the other door to the sally port inside the unit. Wow! What a major screw-up for the institution.

Over the next forty-eight hours, we heard all kinds of rumors. The *Commercial Appeal,* the Memphis newspaper, carried the story the next day in the paper. It was entitled "Inmate Killed." The arti-cle stated the man's name and age. It said he had died from stab wounds. It went on to say he had been stabbed by another inmate. The story said there was a known vendetta between the man that was stabbed and the man that stabbed him. The officials at the prison were quoted as saying they had no idea how the second inmate had gotten out of his cell/cage. It also stated, "The two officers in the unit wrestled with the attacker and drove him back into his cell. At that point, they dragged the stabbed victim into the sally port and sought medical attention for him. The murder weapon was never found. It was assumed it had been flushed down the toilet in the cell by the inmate that did the stabbing."

I was furious and couldn't believe what I had just read. Officer Applewhite (Cockeye) had the murder weapon. I saw it in his hand, dripping blood on the sally port floor. There were not two officers in A-Pod. There was no scuffle between two officers and the inmate that did the stabbing. I didn't know how he got out of his cell, but I knew he couldn't get out unless Ms. Brady popped the electric door.

He had an intercom. I wondered what kind of rouse he used to get her to open his door. It was a huge cover-up by the institution.

The article said the man died before the ambulance arrived at the institution. It said he bled to death. It was as if his life didn't matter. I wondered how scared my family and Keith's family and the other families of the inmates would be when they read an inmate had been stabbed to death. His life did matter. I will never forget him looking me in the eye when I asked him if he was all right. I was offended by the lies and cover up. The prison officials screwed up and couldn't bring themselves to admit it. It was sad. A man had lost his life for nothing! It was revolting! I wished I had access to the man's family. I would have told them the truth. They deserved the truth and still do.

CHAPTER 45

MORE VIOLENCE

The entire compound had been affected by the DC inmate's death. There was a solemn feeling that prevailed during the next few weeks. I knew I would never forget what I had seen and how it made me feel.

One of the big problems in our unit was mealtime. You could go up and get your tray easily enough. Sometimes the officer handed us a tray, and sometimes he just stood back and let us grab our own. He just supervised. He had to because men would take more trays if he didn't watch, or they would take a special vegetable tray or a tray left over because a man was at court or gone out on a medical trip. The real problem was with the drinks. We mentioned before the problem with men scooping ice with their own dirty cup instead of using the clean cup provided. In addition, with the smuggled goods in the bottom of the cooler of ice, someone would distract the guard, and another inmate would just stick his hand and arm down in the ice to retrieve the smuggled goods. In addition, they routinely ran out of Kool-Aid, tea, and ice.

There was another problem at mealtime. Some men just refused to stand in line for a drink or ice. They would just circle around to the front of the line and cut in front of the first inmate that came along that they perceived as weak. By that, I mean someone that wouldn't stand up to them.

I knew I couldn't stand there and let anyone cut line in front of me without responding. I just wasn't made up that way. Also, I knew if a prisoner was ever perceived as weak, he would have many other instances of men trying to take advantage of him. There was a price to pay if he were deemed to be weak and wouldn't stand up for himself. As a result, I just never lined up for a drink or ice. I just waited until there were only three or four men in line and then went up to get mine. If I didn't get a drink, I always had a soda from commissary or water I could drink.

There was a table in the dayroom with four attached metal stools just about five feet from my cell door. I always ate lunch with Keith at that table. Keith had managed to transfer to B-Pod, but we were still not cellmates. I was still in a cell with Nacho. One day at dinner, Keith and I were sitting at the table when the food cart came in with our trays and the drink and ice coolers. Keith and I both went and got a tray and returned to the table. He grabbed his cup and said, "Let's get something to drink." I told him I wasn't going to stand in that line. I would just wait because I didn't want to go through the hassle. I didn't want to get into it over someone trying to cut in front of me.

He said, "I'm going. They aren't going to cut in front of me."

I watched him go line up in the drink/ice line. There were about thirty men already lined up. As Keith moved forward in line and neared the front, a huge young black man named Cleo walked around to the front to cut line. Cleo had only been there about three days. He was about 6 feet 4 inches and 250 pounds. He wasn't over twenty-two or twenty-three years old. He didn't have an ounce of fat on him. He was just a big, young, strong black man.

As Keith stuck his cup under the spout to get his drink, Cleo stepped around from the other side with his cup, pushed Keith's cup out of the way, and tried to get his drink. Keith pushed back. Both had just a little tea in their cups. They continued pushing the cups back and forth. Eventually, they stood up, looked at each other, and both threw their tea in the other man's face at the same time. There was a female officer working the unit that day. She just stood there and watched the entire thing unfold. She didn't say a word until they both threw their tea on the other man. Then, she said, "Hey, stop it! That's enough!"

Cleo walked away. Keith filled up his cup and came back to the table. "That bastard!" he said. I told him, "Keith, I told you something like this would happen. It's just not worth it!"

The line was gone, so I went up and filled up my cup with ice and tea and came back to the table. We ate our dinner in silence. I noticed Cleo never went to his table and sat down. He just stood behind the kiosk, leaning on the concrete and watching everyone else. I saw some of the men in the unit go by and kid with him about the incident and about him being all wet.

Keith said he was going to his cell to get his transcript. He said he found something he wanted to show me. I told him I would take the trays back and go to my room and write Kara a letter. He said he'd come down to my cell in a few minutes. I went into the cell and pulled my door almost closed, but not quite. I didn't want it to lock. I grabbed my Walkman, turned to a sports talk show, and began writing Kara.

I wasn't quite finished with my letter but at least five or ten minutes had passed when a guy from Memphis, AC, came and knocked on my door. I said "Come in" and expected to look up and see Keith walking through my door. AC said, "Did you see what happened to Keith?" I said, "No, what happened?" I could see Keith's back as I looked out through the doorway as he walked toward the sally port. There was an officer walking beside him. My first impression was that Keith had said something smart to an officer and got himself in trouble. I was wrong.

A.C. said, "Cleo went in and beat the hell out of Keith with a combination lock in a sock. Keith was on the floor in his drawer under his cot and had his back to the door. He didn't even know Cleo was behind him. When he turned around, Cleo tore him up. There's blood all over the cell. Keith is really hurt."

I jumped up and ran down to Keith's cell. I hadn't seen that much blood in my life except for the DC inmate that had been stabbed to death. I was really mad. I asked AC, "Where's Cleo now?" He said, "The guards took him out, Coach." I was glad he was gone.

I felt for Keith, but I was also mad at him for going up there when he knew this could be the result. I was concerned for him. I was also mad at myself for not being there to help him. They locked us down and brought in a crew to clean up Keith's cell.

Keith went to the hospital. He had both jaws broken in five places. They had to wire his jaws together. His nose was broken in four places. They took him to medical lockup at 201 Poplar when he left the hospital. In medical isolation there, he was only two blocks from an emergency room at a hospital. They were afraid he might get choked and die. They said he would get used to having his jaws wired, but until then, he would be safer at 201 Poplar's medical isolation unit. I would miss Keith for the next four or five weeks.

Come to find out, Cleo was a violent offender from the state prison. He should never have been in our unit. He was facing federal charges for assaulting a guard at the state prison in Northwest Tennessee. We were all nonviolent offenders. He should have never been in our unit in the first place. Again, the institution had screwed up. It had not cost Keith his life, but he had paid a pretty good price for their screw-up. It had almost cost another man his life!

CHAPTER 46

ADAPTING, ADJUSTING, AND WORKING ON MY CASE

I began a really rewarding correspondence with my aunt Darlene, my dad's only sibling. She and I were so much alike. We seemed to be able to look at each other and know everything about each other without even speaking. It was really incredible. She had a son just eight months younger than me. They had moved away from our hometown when I was young. They also had a daughter about three years younger than me. Our families always spent Christmas Eve together each year but only saw each other a few other times in a typical year.

Her son had been diagnosed with cancer at about thirty-five. He had valiantly fought it for almost ten years. He passed away just about the time I got locked up. Her daughter was getting married and going through some upheavals as well. Also, her husband, Uncle Rob, had a stroke. Aunt Darlene became the primary caregiver. Her life had taken some really tough turns.

Maybe because I was incarcerated and far away or maybe because she and I were so much alike, she felt comfortable confiding in me. Her letters were very open and forthcoming. I was allowed an intimate look into her heart, her life, and her problems. I know I became her confidant. I was the one person she could safely confide in. Our correspondence during my time at Mason was so meaningful to me. I came to love her like never before.

Her mom, my Granny Phillips, became another important pen pal. She as my only living grandparent had never questioned me about my crime or guilt or innocence. I don't think it really mattered to her. She just loved me unconditionally. She was ninety-four years old and still mowed her own yard with a push mower. On her ninety-fifth birthday, she told my dad (her son) she wanted some 10-foot long tree trimming shears for her birthday. She said she had some tree limbs she wanted to cut away. My dad bought her the shears.

In one of her letters, she mentioned she had just finished reading the Bible from cover to cover for the fifteenth time. That was amazing to me. Here I was at forty-seven years old, and I had never actually read the Bible from the front cover to the back cover. I received this letter early in my stay at Mason because I still had the Bible I had picked up that was in two pieces. Over the next twenty-nine days, I read the Bible cover to cover for the first time. Her letters were always so supportive. She encouraged me so much.

Of course, I received letters from Kara, Paul, Jen, and Mom. As I said before, mail call was an important part of each day. We passed the daily Memphis newspaper around all over the unit. The daily papers hung around for weeks at a time.

Paul took a part-time job at one of the largest bookstore chains in the world. Working there, he could purchase books for us at a discount price and have them sent directly to us from the store itself. All our hardcover books had to come directly from the bookstore or publisher or we couldn't receive them. He kept Kara and me supplied with all the latest reading materials. I am sure he didn't make much money working there because he spent all he made, plus some more, buying books for Kara and me. We read everything we could get our hands on.

With Keith gone, September just flew by. I begin to list everything I could think of that was wrong with my case and my trial. It seemed to be a never-ending list. I would think I was finished, but I always found something else. I added to the list almost daily. There was so much wrong! I didn't know how it would help or if it would help, but it certainly was good therapy for me. I wasn't ready to give up. I had never been a quitter. I had always been a fighter. Here is just a partial list of problematic testimony/events from our case:

- Nance's four written statements and his trial testimony all being different clearly showed he had committed perjury.
- Nance's testimony about me buying sodium metal through Bartlett High School was such a sham. I had never worked a day at Bartlett High School. To order that metal, a person had to be a registered authorized buyer. It was a closely controlled substance. Besides, a history teacher (which I was) would have an impossible time trying to buy something that would clearly go through the science department. Also, to buy anything at school, there is a paper trail of requisitions a mile long.
- DEA agent Mike March's testimony to the grand jury was simply lying! It was not a matter of misspeaking.
- In regard to all the trash laying at the edge of the woods and behind the barn that we supposedly couldn't have missed, the Shelby County deputy that was called to the property the day before the fire because of a chemical smell didn't see or notice anything, and he was a trained professional looking for *anything* out of the ordinary.
- The search warrant was completely foul.
- Chain of custody on the evidence was broken when the evidence was not logged in to the appropriate evidence room of the court/judge that signed the warrant. Instead, the evidence was seized by the feds.
- The strip search and questioning of Kara the day of the fire in our bedroom violated her civil rights, including Miranda.
- We were held captive in our own home (handcuffed) illegally when we were *not* under arrest, not free to leave, and watched over by an armed guard.
- The meth in the plastic bucket was clearly a plant because Nance testified there was never any meth cooked and that all the supplies burned up before it became meth.

- The bucket would have melted in the fire.
- The meth in the bucket would have melted in the fire or been dissolved by the water sprayed on the fire by the firemen.
- Nance and Tisdale had both testified about events going on in a building other than the one they were supposedly sleeping in at the time of the fire. That would have been physically impossible.
- Nance testified we were always around when they cooked meth buying supplies, cooking flea powder, Kara washing dishes and cooking food while Nance and Tisdale cooked meth in the barn, even though Tisdale testified we were out of town at the same cooks.
- There was clearly selective and vindictive prosecution on this case since Nance, Tisdale, and Boone had not been charged or prosecuted.
- Nance accusing Kara of providing ether when Tisdale had worked construction jobs and told the authorities in his Missouri case that he stole all the ether he needed from eighteen-wheeler trailers parked at the construction site where he worked.
- Nance's testimony that they had cooked meth there with us in 1994, 1995, May of 1996, May of 1997, and July 13, 1997, the day of the fire. We didn't live there until February of 1996. That rules out the 1994 and 1995 cooks. Tisdale testified he didn't meet Jack Phillips until November of 1996 (and Kara after that), so clearly we could not have cooked meth with Nance and Tisdale in May of 1996. Those three cooks (1994, 1995, and May of 1996) could not have occurred. We were wrongly charged with those crimes and the meth produced at each.
- DEA agent March testifying that R. A. Boone was not at court because they couldn't find him when in fact they had not even looked for him even though Nance and Tisdale testified he was cooking meth when the fire started.

- The AUSA misleading the jury and making it sound as if Jack had coached Sam Nance in high school football when Jack had never coached a high school game of football in the state of Arkansas.
- The card from Timmy Tisdale stating that Sam Nance was going to lie to the authorities.
- All the statements we had gathered from the inmates where Nance and Tisdale bragged about getting out of trouble by dragging a teacher and his wife into the case.

I knew I would come up with some more later. However, this seemed like an awful lot and an impressive list. It clearly revealed that Nance and Tisdale were liars. I wondered how many lies constituted perjury in the eyes of the law? I copied all of these things down in detail and sent copies to Paul, Lester Moore, and June Riley.

Paul told me he had talked to Lester Moore. He said Lester had given the okay for Phillip Watson, the attorney and old football player of ours, to come to Mason and take sworn statements from the men that had given statements to me about what they had heard Nance and Tisdale say. I had thirteen letters in my possession. They had bragged an awful lot about setting us up. In late September, we got the sworn affidavits from all the men.

Keith returned to Mason October 3, 1998. His jaws were still wired together. He had lost about forty pounds since I had seen him. They still had to put all his food in a blender so he could take it in through a straw. It was good to see him, but I sure felt sorry for him. Having your jaws wired together was really tough.

They put him in B-Pod with us. There was an empty cell in B-Pod, so I went and ask the counselor if I could move in with Keith. She said it was all right, so I packed my stuff up, said good-bye to Nacho, and moved three doors down into a cell with Keith. Keith was supposed to go back to the hospital in two weeks to get the wires removed. There was one thing that was clearly different about Keith besides the weight loss: he snored now. His nose had been reset, but obviously there were still some problems. Even with the solid metal door, we could hear him snoring all the way out in the dayroom. He had never snored before. Thank God for earplugs!

CHAPTER 47

A NEW SENTENCING DATE AND KEITH

Paul tried to reach Lester Moore. It seemed it was getting harder and harder to get the attorneys to talk to any of us. I had written letters to both Lester and June. All had gone unanswered. We began to feel as if they were through with us. I tried to call all the numbers I had for Lester and never got an answer. I had not received any communication from him at all. Kara had had the same problem with June Riley. She hadn't spoken to her or seen her one time. It had reached the point where it appeared she wasn't taking Kara's calls either.

Paul had become more determined than ever to speak to Lester. He had repeatedly called and been told Lester wasn't in the office. On one occasion, Paul called and was told Lester wasn't in, so he just drove over to his office and parked in the back of the parking lot and sat and waited. He watched Lester pull up in his Mercedes Benz, park, get out, and go in the back door of his office. Paul called his office on his mobile phone and was told Lester was not in. While he was speaking to the secretary, he was walking to the back office door Lester had just entered. While still on the phone, he entered the office itself. When the secretary looked up and saw him, she got really red-faced. Paul told her, "I just saw him come in, yet you are constantly telling me he's not here. I'm not leaving until I talk to him."

She got up and said "Just a minute" and headed down the hall. In a moment, she returned and said, "Mr. Moore will see you now, Mr. Phillips. Go right back to the office on the right."

This meeting wasn't pretty. Paul accused Lester of avoiding him and us and of giving up on the case. Lester basically told Paul that he was bothering him and he didn't have time to talk to him or deal with him. That was the wrong thing to say to Paul.

Paul got with Lester quickly. He told him, "You are Jack's lawyer. You should be helping him. You won't even respond to his requests to talk to you fifteen minutes on the phone. Jack will never quit fighting this injustice. If you won't talk to him, you will have to talk to me."

Lester said, "I don't have time to deal with any of you."

Paul said, "Look, just tell me what it's going to take to get Jack and Kara out of this mess. What's it going to take?"

Lester told him, "The only thing that could get them out is if you could get someone who was involved in the meth cooking that would be willing to say they weren't involved. That's really the only way."

Paul told Lester, "Then that is what we will do!"

About the only new information we had was that our sentencing date had been moved from November to December 5, 1998. We had to refocus our mind-set on a different date. It meant I would be at Mason and Kara would be at Hardeman County for at least an additional month. It meant it would be at least another month until we could see each other. Paul did give Lester a copy of the sheet I had already sent him of the discrepancies in our case.

Later the same week, Paul had a similar experience with June Riley, Kara's attorney. She was so distracted by her caseload it was obvious we weren't going to get much from her. She had moved on to other cases. She did promise Paul she would communicate more regularly with Kara in the future.

Kara and I both had visits. Kara's visits were noncontact. That is, she had to visit with a glass separating her from her visitors. I had contact visits. We all sat around a table and could shake hands and hug one another when we arrived and left. Kara and I continued our nightly talks at 6:00 p.m. I was grateful that Cockroach had moved to B-Pod the same time I did. He ran the phones in B-Pod just like he had in A-Pod. I thanked God for Cockroach every day!

By the end of October, it was obvious Keith wasn't going to get any help. Almost a month passed and he still had not been taken back to the hospital. One of the vertical wires holding his jaws together on one side had already broken. The right side held firmly. Keith's gums were beginning to grow over the wires wrapped around each tooth, top and bottom. By the second week in November, Keith had taken fingernail clippers and clipped the other vertical wire. He could now eat food. His mouth was slightly crooked from the tension on the one wire on the right side. Had it been removed on time, there is no doubt his mouth wouldn't be twisted. At least he could eat. He began gaining some of the weight he had lost. He started looking like his old self except for that twisted mouth. He still needed to get the wires out that encircled each tooth individually on the top and bottom of his mouth.

We began to prepare for Thanksgiving. Labor Day had come and gone. That was hard because Kara and I had been surrounded by family and friends on the Fourth of July and Memorial Day. We missed everyone connected to the Labor Day holiday. Thanksgiving would be even harder because it was such a family-oriented holiday. Our family (daughter, son, and grandchildren) and Paul, Jen, and their son were having a difficult time figuring out where to have Thanksgiving. It had always been at Mom and Dad's house. Now, they were in Memphis. It wouldn't be at their house in Rector for the first time in our entire lives. Our absence would be magnified when the family all got together. Kara's family would be gathered at her mom's house in Rector. Our absence would be felt there as well. All in all, it didn't look like a very promising holiday.

CHAPTER 48

MS. CAIN AND OFFICER MCDANIEL

There were two female officers that had a great impact on my stay at Mason. They were Officers Cain and McDaniel. Ms. Cain was a fifty-something-year-old female officer as cool as the other side of the pillow. She had a natural sassiness about her that belied her age. Simply put, she was a flirt, but not in any vulgar sort of way.

Ms. Cain used to be our evening officer. Her shift ran from 4:00 p.m. until midnight. Then she moved to the midnight to 8:00 a.m. shift. She almost always worked our pod. It wasn't unusual to be taking a shower in the open stall and see Ms. Cain standing there. Often she would conduct a conversation with you as you stood stark-naked, showering openly in front of her (about twelve feet away). It was really embarrassing at first, but you got used to seeing her in the unit, and then there was Ms. Brady in the control room bubble. Both could see everything! I spent more time nude in front of those two women than any other woman I had ever met, except for Kara. Over the course of time, it just didn't matter if they were watching or not. A prisoner learned to take that in stride too and just move on.

Ms. McDaniel was a blond in her twenties. She was a little overweight and not bad looking, but not what a person would call naturally beautiful. However, she did have a great smile and a good personality that made her attractive. I don't remember her ever talking to inmates while they showered like Ms. Cain. Keith and I both called her Linda when we were talking to her alone. She didn't mind at all and preferred it actually. When anyone else was around, we called her Officer McDaniel.

Starting shortly after Keith returned from 201 Poplar, Ms. Cain and Linda began showing up at our pod after we were locked in each night at 10:30 p.m. They had the officer in the bubble pop our door. We went into the dayroom, carry one of the tables over under the stairway so it couldn't be seen from the hallway, and then sit and talk to them for hours at a time. Sometimes we sat out there all night. They brought us drinks and snacks from the vending machines in the officers' lounge. If we needed colored pens or items we couldn't get at the commissary, they brought them in for us too. Anything we needed to work on our case, they would provide. They never brought us contraband or immoral merchandise.

There was never any inappropriate contact either, but there was some flirting, joke telling, and laughing. Actually, we had a great time and looked forward to our get-together each night. We had so much fun with those two officers, and I am sure it broke the monotony of working there for them. After a few weeks, we had come to know a great deal about them, and they knew a great deal about us.

Ms. Cain had gotten her twenty-one-year-old daughter a job at the facility. We had been introduced to her. She was simply a knockout! Wow! She was stunningly beautiful. She hadn't worked there a month until she was caught having sex with one of the Montana inmates. She was instantly fired. When we heard the story about the female guard, at first we weren't told it was Ms. Cain's daughter.

Both of the officers knew everything there was to know about our cases. They empathized with us and said it was obvious to them we were not criminals. They told us on many occasions they knew we did not belong there. That meant a lot to Keith and me.

The Bible studies I had been teaching continued to grow. More and more men came. At times, we had to hold them in the dayroom because we couldn't get all the men into our cell. Officers Cain and

McDaniel often came by and sat in for a while. The church was prospering there too. I began to read scriptures occasionally and even do words of encouragement at the services when asked.

Paul sent in some appropriate scriptures for our situation he had printed off his computer on fancy paper. They were beautiful, relevant scriptures. They were taped all around the walls of the classroom where we had church. We had anywhere from twenty to forty men attending all our services. We were packed into that room for the Tuesday night service and a Sunday morning service. The prison staff really didn't like so many inmates assembling together. They always thought we must be passing contraband (that never happened). The staff decided to do something about it.

First, they removed all the plastic chairs from the room. We tried to find out why, but no one would say why it happened. We were never given an explanation. The numbers, however, did not decline. In fact, the number of those who came increased as we all just sat on the floor. We started bringing our blankets to sit on them so it wasn't so hard, but they stopped that. The inmates kept showing up for church anyway.

Secondly, they cranked up the heat. When removing the chairs didn't work, they turned up the heat on the thermostat, which was locked in a box on the wall so we couldn't get to it. One Tuesday night we showed up for church, and it must have been 120 degrees in the room. It was like Daniel in the fiery furnace! Although it was November and cold outside, we worshiped and dripped sweat!

Thirdly, when that didn't work, they just turned the heat completely off. They wouldn't let us take our blankets or wear our jackets or sweatshirts. We had to wear the short-sleeved institutional shirt to go to church. Again, the man just kept coming at us!

During the first week in December, the chairs were returned and the thermostat set to a reasonable reading. We seemed to have won that battle. We all felt like we had suffered for the Lord's sake a little and endured the tests he had set before us. In fact, it seemed the more they did, the more the church prospered. I was proud to be part of that church. It was a real church!

CHAPTER 49

PRESENTENCE INVESTIGATION REPORT

I received a letter from Lester Moore informing me that a person from the probation office would be coming to do a presentence report on me. I didn't even know what that was. The letter said she would arrive on Tuesday, the second week of November, at 1:00 p.m. Lester said he would be there too to advise me when she did the report.

I had no idea of the significance of the presentence report since Lester said he would be there too, so I gave the matter no further thought. No one had ever mentioned a presentence investigative report to me.

When the day rolled around, I was called over the intercom to report to a small office often used for lawyer conferences to meet with the probation officer. The officer was a nice-looking lady who smiled and seemed rather intelligent. She had an outgoing personality and was easy with people. She began a conversation with me the moment I entered the room. She asked if my attorney was coming and whom he or she was. I told her it was Lester Moore and that he said he would be there for the meeting. She said she knew Lester real well and we would wait for him to arrive. We sat and chatted until

1:30 p.m. She finally said, "We have to begin. I have to get back to Memphis."

That didn't bother me. I figured Lester would show up sooner or later. I told her, "Okay, let's do it."

She began by asking me about my family and background. We went through everything from my family, elementary school, and junior high. We must have spent thirty minutes alone on my high school years, sports, and the relationship between Kara and me. We went into our marriage, college years, and our children and grand-children. She asked about arrests as a juvenile or an adult. Just the type of questions I expected her to ask.

We finally got around to my teaching/coaching career and the various places we had lived and worked. I gave her a list of all the places Kara had worked too. She asked about our financial history and condition, and I told her. She wanted to know a lot about the two companies we had owned and ran with Paul and the strength coach at Memphis State University from 1991–1995. We also had a Russian partner who had immigrated here. He had a doctorate degree in human speed development. He had created a program running with small parachutes to improve speed. We marketed those and did really well. We started a second company to market specialty devices and nutritional supplements. We actually made a lot of money. She was surprised I would leave the good money and return to teaching and coaching. She had no idea that teaching and coaching were a calling and something that was or was not in your blood. It was in my blood. The money I made in the companies did not bring me the joy I got from teaching and coaching.

She asked about drugs and alcohol, and I admitted experiment-ing with both in the early seventies during my college years. I was able to tell her no, there were no alcohol or drug problems in either of our lives. Our jobs were too demanding, and we were too commit-ted to our families to be involved with drugs or alcohol.

She grilled me about our finances. We were over our heads in debt. She didn't seem to be able to grasp that (or didn't want to). We lived paycheck to paycheck and always had. Sometimes there wasn't enough money to pay every bill. We had no savings, didn't own our home or any property, didn't own our car, and didn't live above our means. We barely squeaked by!

She asked about my version about what happened regarding the crime. I briefly went through all that with her. She didn't take notes on that. I asked her if she would be talking to Kara too. She said a probation officer would be visiting her to talk to her, but it would be someone other than her.

It was almost 3:30 p.m. when Lester Moore finally walked in. She had already put up her pad, recorder, and pen. He asked me how it went, and I told him, "Fine, I guess." Lester and she exchanged pleasantries and seemed very familiar with each other.

She gave me her card, shook my hand, said good-bye, and left. She thanked me on her way out. Lester took my hand and shook it and asked how things were going.

I told him, "Lester, I wish you had been here, but that's done and over with. I do want you to promise me one thing."

He said, "What's that?"

I told him, "When we come to sentencing, I want you and June to make sure you take time to talk privately with Kara and me so we can have ten or fifteen minutes together. I may not see her for a long time, and it's really important to both of us to have just a few last minutes together. Will you promise me that?"

He said, "I will promise you that. Anything else?"

I said, "How about subpoenas for some of the men who wrote the affidavits so they can come testify at sentencing?"

He said, "They won't let us retry the case, Jack."

I told him, "I know that, but let's at least give Judge Burns a chance to hear what is being said by Nance and Tisdale."

He said, "Okay, I'll try to get them to let one or two of them come."

"At least get Keith Hawkins there," I told him. "He has good information and will be good on the stand."

"Okay," he said and then added, "I have to go, but I'll be back to see you before sentencing."

I thanked him and returned to my unit. He and the lady left together and went down the hallway in the other direction.

Two nights later, I found out from Kara when I called home that a large black lady from the probation office had been over to see her. She related the experience, and it sounded identical to mine. I had been feeling pretty good about my meeting, and I felt pretty good about hers. We had nothing to hide. June Riley did show up for Kara's meeting. I was a little upset that Lester had not shown up for mine.

I was anxious for the sentencing hearing. Maybe with Keith's testimony and the affidavits, we could get through to the judge. I had another one in the hole too. Lester had told Paul to contact everyone he could think of to write letters on our behalf. Paul assured me a very large number of people had promised to write letters. He had contacted alumni associations from all the schools where we had worked. He had contacted family and friends and associates from across the country. I knew we had some passionate supporters that would declare and guarantee our innocence.

We felt about the same as we had felt before the trial. We needed resolution. This had been hanging over our head for over fifteen months. We were both worn out from worrying. As the saying goes, "We were sick and tired of being sick and tired." We didn't want to go to real prison, but we did need closure. We still felt we had a chance to reverse things and win!

CHAPTER 50

PRESENTENCE REPORT REVEALED

aul talked to Lester Moore and learned our sentencing would indeed be held on December 5, 1998. It had not been moved again. Phillip Watson, the attorney helping Paul, agreed to come to Court for the sentencing with Paul to see what was going on. He had already read all the discovery and had been through the transcripts. He had taken the affidavits. The transcript had been a real disappointment to me. It was only 80 percent to 85 percent accurate at best. Much was simply missing. That, however, wasn't the biggest problem we faced.

We finally received the presentence investigative report (called the PSI or PSR) written by the lady probation officer. It was unbelievable. For instance, the report included eight or ten pages of paragraphed materials from a statement made by Sam Nance. It was the statement of January 27, 1998. This was before our trial in August 1998. This particular statement was given just four days prior to the grand jury convening that indicted us for the crime. I speculated that this was probably the same testimony Nance had given the grand jury. If I was on that grand jury and had heard that statement, I would have indicted us too.

The problem I had with it was that it was *not* what Sam Nance had testified to at trial. I guess the probation officer concluded that since this was the last written statement Nance had given, it must be accurate and be the same as his testimony at trial. Not only was it different from what he had testified to at trial, it was different from the other three written (sworn) depositions he had given. I couldn't believe she had included it in the report as fact. In this statement, he said that he and Timmy Tisdale were cooking the meth when he made a mistake that caused a small explosion and resulted in the fire. He never mentioned R. A. Boone. There were other equally disturbing contradictions. In court, he said that he and Timmy Tisdale were sleeping when the fire broke out. This statement was presented as fact in this report! *What about R. A. Boone?* I wondered.

Even more disturbing was a statement in this report from Timmy Tisdale! The government had been adamant during the trial that there was no statement (not even notes) from anything Timmy Tisdale said. Yet here, dated January 28, 1998, just one day after Nance's statement and three days before the grand jury hearing is a statement from Tisdale! Tisdale also claimed he and Nance were cooking meth when the fire started. No mention here either of R. A. Boone. It was full of inconsistencies. At trial, he testified he was asleep on the couch in the house when the fire started and R. A. Boone was cooking meth. How could these be presented in this report as factual when neither Tisdale nor Nance testified to any of it at trial? Was I being judged by these written statements (one of which, Tisdale's, was not even supposed to exist) or by their trial testimony? I was shocked the presentence investigative report was so shabby.

There were other surprises too. I saw I was not only going to be sentenced for the three counts for which I had been convicted, but I was also going to be enhanced (given more time) two points for obstruction of justice for allegedly trying to prevent the firemen from fighting the fire. I had not been found guilty of that! Two points meant three to five additional years! I was also enhanced three points for "endangering human life while manufacturing." The problem with this was the mandatory minimum for the three counts I had been convicted of already carried ten years for count one, twenty years for count two, and ten years for count three. That was a total of *forty years* before the enhancements!

It showed my level on the sentencing table at level 34. With the enhancements, I would be at level 39. The sentencing for level 34 was 110–168 months. For level 39, the sentencing table said 262–327 months! I was really upset. I had not been convicted by the jury of obstructing justice! This lady had arbitrarily in my mind convicted me in this PSI. As for the endangering human life enhancement, I had already been convicted of that, and it carried a twenty-year sentence. It seemed as if I was being doubly punished for the same thing! It was going to cost me my very life! At forty-seven, I couldn't do that much time and come out alive!

Besides, I had never obstructed those firemen. The firemen couldn't even identify me as the white male at the fire. They had received twenty-three calls at 911 about the fire. The first one came from my phone! I had four small gas cans for the lawnmower. If I was guilty, I would have poured the gasoline on the fire and burned the barn to the ground and they would never have discovered a meth lab. I could have blocked the driveway with the two cars at my house and the firemen couldn't have gotten to the fire to fight it. The structure would have burned down. I had sprayed water on the fire with my water hoses until they got there. Everything I had done was exactly what an innocent person would do in that same situation. Now, I was accused of obstructing the firemen!

I called Paul and had him call Lester and June. I knew if my presentence report was screwed up, then Kara's would be too. I told Paul to tell Lester and June we were objecting to everything in the presentence report beyond our background and work information. That attractive, intelligent probation officer was nothing more than a wolf in sheep's clothing. Although I hadn't yet been sentenced, I got a good look at what I was facing. She had done the calculations. It was frightening! That lady was completely incompetent to be determining the rest of our lives. Where did she get the constitutional authority to make such decisions about our fate? She had drawn conclusions that would dramatically affect the rest of our lives.

Keith got a subpoena and was licking his chops to testify. Most importantly, it was about time for me to see Kara again. I had missed her beyond what words could express!

CHAPTER 51

SENTENCING

Finally, the day arrived for sentencing. It was December 5, 1998. I would get to see Kara. I had written Lester a fifteen-page account of what was wrong with the presentence report. I had copied the report and marked it all up. I had not heard a reply from Lester.

The morning of sentencing, they woke Keith and me up at 2:00 a.m. We were placed in the holding cell in the little office. There were three other inmates in there with us who were also going to court that day. We didn't leave Mason until 7:45 a.m. The time passed quickly as we reviewed all that might occur in court. I was extremely anxious. Keith was glad to be going and looking forward to testifying. Descussio had taken a sailing class from Keith years before and owed Keith $480, which he had failed to pay. Keith was looking forward to going up against Descussio in court.

I was looking forward to the fifteen minutes with Kara so we could talk over some things that needed to be said face-to-face. We arrived about 8:35 a.m. I didn't see Lester until about 8:45 a.m. He said Kara hadn't arrived at the courthouse yet, but he assured me he would make certain that we got our time together even if it was after the hearing.

We entered the courtroom at about 8:55 a.m. Kara came in at 9:00 a.m. on the dot. We hugged and hugged. She looked great. We both cried a little too. I couldn't take my eyes off her. We settled in, and the judge arrived and called the proceeding to order.

The first order of business was the presentence report. The judge asked Kara if she had read the report and had time to discuss it with her attorney, June Riley. Kara answered "Yes, sir" to both questions.

He asked me the same questions, and I responded, "Yes, sir. I have read it."

The judge wasn't satisfied with my answer. He asked me, "Have you studied it and discussed it with your attorney, Mr. Phillips?"

I told him, "I've studied it and corresponded with my attorney through the mail about some on it." The rest of the conversation was recorded in the court transcript:

> **Court:** Are you telling me you've fully discussed it with him by mail?
>
> **Mr. Phillips:** Well, I sent him what I thought were some things that needed to be changed in it, but I never heard anything back. I haven't had a conversation with him since.
>
> **Court:** Are you telling me you're not ready to proceed?
>
> **Mr. Moore:** Your Honor, so the record will be clear, Mr. Phillips sent me a fifteen page handwritten document, and in that he brings up several items and inquiries. He said, "I'm not sure whether this relates to a motion for a new trial or whether this relates to sentencing, but these are my thoughts and considerations." Of those that I thought would clearly apply to sentencing, we have noted them in response or position to the sentencing. As to the other items, I advised Mr. Phillips before Your Honor came out that those items which I think more clearly address a motion for a new trial or other motions that do not relate to the sentencing report itself. That is, at this point the Court may treat the jury verdict—the jury verdict is not a retrial of the fact of the case.
>
> **Court:** Do you understand that?
>
> **Mr. Phillips:** Yes, sir.

Court: Are you ready to proceed?

Mr. Phillips: Yes, sir. I have no experience here.

Court: Well, I understand that. I just want to hear from your own lips that you have discussed these questions that have arisen in your mind regarding the presentence report with your attorney. You've indicated you have done so by mail. Your attorney obviously got those and filed a petition on your behalf to the presentence report. The government has indicated that it has no objections to the presentence report in both cases or I should say in regard to both defendants. This is correct, is it not?

Mr. Descussio: That is correct Your Honor.

At this point, Lester Moore argued the idea that I had interfered with the firemen in regard to the obstruction of justice enhancement in the presentence report. He pointed out that at trial, none of the firefighters could identify me as being there or saying or doing anything. Here is the response to Lester's argument, however convoluted it might be, from the AUSA:

Mr. Descussio: Your Honor, at trial, it was discussed, Mr. Phillips was the—you know, he lived there, Your Honor.

The next thing Lester brought up was the drug amounts. Nance was the only one that stated anything about amounts. The point was made that the testimony by one of the firemen was that there were fifty to sixty empty cans of ether. That is not enough to cook five pounds of meth, as Mr. Nance claims and for which the Phillips were going to be sentenced.

Court: Mr. Descussio?

Mr. Descussio: Well, Your Honor, we, of course, had a lot of trial testimony and the trial testimony is supported by the findings that—that the officer made in the presentence report and we stand by these—that testimony given in Court.

It was amazing that a trained, experienced, and educated AUSA could speak in such broken and fragmented English and not have one person ask, "What is he talking about?" His responses sounded like gibberish to everyone in the court except the judge, apparently. Maybe he could understand him. I don't know how. Kara's and my sentence were being determined to a great degree from the presentence report made by people that must not have even been at the trial. I ask, How can that be fair or just? How can the probation officers exercise that much power? Do they have any real constitutional power to determine our sentences? I think not!

Court: Mr. Moore, do you wish to put any proof with regard to that objection?

Mr. Moore: Let me ask Mr. Phillips.

I told Lester to put Keith on the stand. He will blow Nance and Tisdale's credibility out of the water. There ensued a lengthy discussion of the relevance of Keith's testimony in regard to drug amounts. I felt anything related to Nance's credibility had relevance. The judge overruled the objection as his testimony and amounts. We lost again.

Lester argued that I played a minimal role and should be treated as a minimal participant. The judge overruled that objection too. Judge Burns moved on to June Riley.

Court: All right, Ms. Riley, does your client have objections to the presentence report?

Ms. Riley: Yes, Your Honor.

Court: Will you state your objections?

June objected to the drug amounts too. She said the calculation could not be proven (same argument Lester had made). She asked Kara to be treated as a minimal participant. She asked for a five-point reduction in her sentence. The court overruled that objection. June wanted her objection noted for appeal purposes. June did manage to get on important fact on the record.

Ms. Riley: But, Your Honor, the jury wasn't asked to make any findings with respect to the amounts.

Court: No, but I cannot—if I disregard his testimony with respect to any one incident, I have effectively disregarded his testimony with respect to all the incidents and therefore I have nullified the verdict. I understand Mr. Nance's testimony is subject to serious attack. He's a criminal, he stands to gain some reduction in sentence by virtue of his plea agreement and following his testimony and I understand the problem with that, but I also know my job is not to determine the credibility of the witness at trial. In our system, that's left to the jury, and that's the way it ought to be.

Who could argue with that? However, the judge just made an assumption that there was/is a plea agreement. He assumed it was common knowledge that Nance and Tisdale testified to gain a reduction in their sentence from Missouri and in an effort to avoid prosecution (with immunity) in the current case. He assumed the jury knew all that and arrived at a fair, just, reasonable conclusion that Nance and Tisdale were credible. However, the jury had learned just the opposite. They heard that Nance and Tisdale had no deal and were getting nothing for their testimony. June Riley was shining like a bright star!

Ms. Riley: I differ with the Court in that respect. We didn't have exactly—in fact, one of the Court's instructions when instructing the jurors in considering evidence is usually that they could accept or reject any or all parts of a person's testimony and we don't know whether they choose to believe all of Mr. Nance's testimony or not.

Court: Well, that is true, although I will have to tell you I think of no logical basis why they would have accepted part of it but not the rest of it because the attack on his credibility went to the total story he was testifying to and not to particular incidents.

The judge said he wasn't ruling on that yet. He said he wanted to hear Mr. Hawkins (Keith) since we had brought him to court. The judge sounded like the AUSA. The judge seemed to sense he had dug a hole for himself concerning the drug amounts. This was probably the highlight of June Riley's career.

Court: I am not saying that as a matter of law I'm bound to tie her (Kara) to every incident that Nance testified. What I am saying is that in this instance, if you accept his testimony of the defendant's participation in the offense, there is no basis I can ascertain to reject his testimony with respect to any other particular incident he testified about, and I have some serious concerns about saying, all right, the jury found the defendants guilty. Obviously, it was largely based—substantially based—on Mr. Nance's testimony, now the Court is going to find that he had no credibility and therefore the defendants should not be held accountable for any of the drugs he said he manufactured with them. And that is what I think you're asking me to do.

That was a pretty good layout of our objection to the proceedings. If the court was so worried about us being held accountable for drugs we manufactured with Nance, where was the judge's concern for holding Nance, Tisdale, and R. A. Boone accountable for the drugs he himself said we manufactured together? What penalty will Nance pay? What penalty will Tisdale pay? What penalty will R.A. Boone pay? Should Nance and Tisdale go unpunished here because they went to Missouri and committed a second crime of manufacturing meth just nine days after the fire in Bartlett? How can they be rewarded by not paying a penalty in this case and committing a second felony elsewhere? The judge has become so blinded by the breakdown in our system that he can't see the injustice in this and can't see clearly and logically. If you don't think the wheels have come off the wagon, just read the next exchange from the transcript that took place between Judge Burns and Terry Descussio, the AUSA.

Court: Okay. Mr. Descussio, there's a substantial body of law out there for sentencing purposes, I'm to make my own factual determination. Ms. Riley is saying that Mr. Nance's testimony was totally incredible and given the plea agreement strongly suspect. In a moment, we are going to hear from Mr. Hawkins. Of course, you are going to have the opportunity to cross examine him.

Mr. Descussio: Your Honor, I'll be happy to cross examine—

Court: Wait a minute. Wait a minute. Is your contention that I am in no way bound by the verdict of the jury with respect to the total amount of drugs charged against the—or calculated against these defendants?

Mr. Descussio: No, I believe that the Court makes the determination independent of the jury verdict. That's a sentencing issue that I believe the Court finds and I agree with that. I mean, I think of I'm—the jury verdict in terms of what the defense was. If they are going to put on some other proof to say these people were involved in another amount, then the Court is going to have to make some sort of determination, I guess, on whether considering—well, number one, Mr. Nance didn't have a plea agreement with us or anybody else, if the Court will recall. He's been convicted and sitting in jail, there's no plea agreement that affects us whatsoever.

Court: I thought I recalled that there was a significant, possibility of a Rule 35.

Mr. Descussio: That may be, but that's just a matter of—I mean, if Mr. Nance testified. He hasn't been promised anything, that's just a matter of the law allows the government to make Rule 35 based on substantial cooperation.

Court: And so are we to think Mr. Nance just came down and testified out of the goodness of his heart?

Mr. Descussio: No, it was up in Missouri. That in and of itself is a reason to believe Mr. Nance because what he in fact did was come down here and involve himself in a whole bunch more methamphetamine than he otherwise was involved with. He was sentenced on the case up in Missouri, and in effect has exposed himself to greater punishment or greater range of punishment by admitting the additional methamphetamine—I'm sure—methamphetamine up in Missouri. The Court might want to find that he's just slightly corroborated by the fact that this operation took place in the defendant's presence at their residence in a shed above their hot tub with equipment and methamphetamine located in their house. Now the Court may find just slightly corroborative of Mr. Nance—

Court: Don't get—

Mr. Descussio: I would tell the Court—

Court: Mr. Descussio, don't get sarcastic.

Mr. Descussio: I'm not. I'm not, but I'm just saying that counsel is sitting here saying well, we're just going to put Mr. Hawkins up there to say, you know, Nance told me he was lying and that ought to just throw Mr. Nance's testimony out. I believe it is a preposterous situation. I think the Court ought to consider more than that, and I think the Court has to consider, number one, the jury finding, and number two, the entire—and the Court heard—the entire case. The Court heard the fact that there were hundreds of thousands of packages of Sudafedrin located in the garbage and in the barrel in back of the house. You know, all the things the Court heard during the case allows the Court to make whatever determination it has. We have—the only proof we have in terms of specific amounts are through Mr. Nance and Mr. Tisdale. These are the only people that were involved in this conspiracy that testified. If they are going to

put on proof on by other people then the Court will
have to weigh it.

Court: Ms. Riley, do you wish to put on any proof with
respect to these objections?

Ms. Riley: No, Your Honor. If I can respond very briefly? I
think you made clear when Mr. Nance testified that
he knew he wasn't going to be prosecuted for this
case. Now, maybe I misunderstood, but I thought
that's what Mr. Nance's understanding was and so he
was saved from—

Court: Well, the record will reflect with a great degree of
accuracy exactly what Mr. Nance said he was expecting in return for his testimony, or as a result of his
testimony, we need not dwell too much on the exact
details. It's—go ahead, anything else?

Ms. Riley: With regard to how much of these pill packages were
found. I think that the Court might recall that when
the officers testified that his grand jury testimony
turned out it was somewhat exaggerated as to the
number of packages that were actually found. There
was some correction that finally came out at trial, of
course, but the Phillips were still convicted. But as
far as the numbers, I think the testimony needs to be
looked at, too, to get a more accurate reflection of the
total amount.

Court: Bring Mr. Hawkins out, would you, Marshall? Swear
in Mr. Hawkins, would you, please?

Keith Hawkins was sworn in, and it was decided that June Riley
would go first. It was revealed that Mr. Hawkins's lawyer was present.
It seemed he had warned Keith of potential problems with testifying,
but Keith had told his attorney his testimony was truthful, and he
was going to testify.

Keith testified that Nance had told him personally that it had
gotten too hot in Missouri, so he and a friend found some people in
the Memphis area who were going to be gone a lot in the summer.
He said Nance told him that there was an old barn or shed on the

property, and he was going to cook meth there when they were gone. He said Nance told him that he and his friend were cooking meth in the old barn when a fire started so they ran.

Nance went on and told Keith that the AUSA had assured him if he testified against the Phillipses, he would get his time reduced on his sentence in Missouri. He said Nance told him, "Well, it was going to be either them or me, and it was not going to be me, baby!"

Keith said Nance told him he wasn't worried about lying because he was a government witness and had immunity. Keith finished up his testimony by relating that he began playing volleyball after his conversation with Nance. June passed the witness to Lester Moore after having Keith tell about his own conviction in his case.

Lester basically got in the fact that Keith had never met me or Kara prior to meeting me at CCA in Mason. He had not been promised anything for his testimony. He knew if he was lying he could face perjury charges, and Mr. Nance had told him a prisoner could get your time cut for testifying against other people.

Terry Descussio then got to cross-examine Keith. He tried to corner Keith on the fact that Keith thought everybody in government lied, that he thought the tapes in his case had been altered, and that he thought his transcript was missing key pieces of information. Keith handled himself extremely well. June Riley was allowed to redirect.

> **Ms. Riley:** You had a conversation with Mr. Nance where you said to him, where you asked him about accusing innocent people, is that right?
>
> **Mr. Hawkins:** That is correct.
>
> **Ms. Riley:** And he responded, how?
>
> **Mr. Hawkins:** He was very cavalier, very aloof and very obnoxious and he said it was either going to be him—him or the other people, and that he had made a deal with the government and prosecution to get his time cut, and he said that was basically the way to go.
>
> **Ms. Riley:** Thank you.

Keith was excused. His testimony was riveting and certainly had the ring of truth to it. Besides, he had also mentioned there were other men (he called three by name) who could verify his testimony. These were men from CCA Mason. We had their affidavits. The men he mentioned were two black men and one white man.

There was then a discussion about the date of the alleged cooks. Although the first three—the 1994, 1995, and May of 1996 cooks—were thrown out after a short break by the court to check the records, it does not appear in the transcript and is not reflected or mentioned in the sentencing computation sheet in the presentence report. It was omitted.

The best way to review the rest of the sentencing hearing is to just quote from the transcript itself.

STATEMENTS FROM THE HEART AT SENTENCING (PAUL PHILLIPS)

Mr. Moore: Your Honor, Mr. Paul Phillips would like to be heard by the Court.

Court: I'd like to hear from Mr. Phillips. I have his letter of course, and I've heard your testimony and I have, as I will indicate in a moment, a number of other letters, and if you want—come on, now, come on up here and you can just stand right here if you want.

Mr. Paul Phillips: This man and I are unusual brothers. We are much closer than brothers, I describe us more like twins, more like identical twins. For the past—since 1975 the past twenty-three years, we've called each other every morning at 5:00 AM to make sure we get up and go to school on time. We've spent our whole lives, Your Honor, working with young people. We worked drug clinics with the DEA, with the drug people out of Shelby County. I had a foster son who was murdered in Kansas City by the Jamaican drug gangs. The last thing anybody in the world anybody in the family would do is touch this stuff. The man's—this man's spent six months of his life working on food supplements, nutritional food supplements, because we were concerned with young athletes using steroids and we travelled through six states speaking to schools and athletes telling them what to stay away from.

I've got two parents—we've got two parents—they're seventy-three years old. My mother has been hospitalized for the third time since August. She's a strong lady. This concern we've had for other people comes out of her concern and teaching about things we ought to do. We're not perfect, we've made mistakes all our lives, all of us, so does everybody in this room. We've had an open-door policy at my house. I was probably the first one outside of my parents and to date we've stood in court with lots of people, we've buried a lot of our athletes. We believed in this justice system. We taught it in schools. For twenty-five years I've taught it in schools portraying that there is justice, and I know we live in a society where when a crime is committed our people want to see somebody pay for it, but that's not justice if it's not the right people paying for it.

Court: There's no question about that.

Mr. Paul Phillips: As a matter of fact, it's a greater injustice. I heard a warden say the other day that ten percent of the people in his institution that he maintains in institutions around the country are innocent. That sounds like an almost acceptable number in our society. That's what we have to do to get those that are guilty. That is not acceptable.

I stand a chance by Christmas—we do—of not having either one of these parents. My dad is a stroke victim. I sat in the Court during the trial—or I couldn't get in here, I testified a little bit. I stood in the windows and I watched people stand up here that my brother sat at my house and wept over and said they're throw away people that nobody wants. Nobody wants them. Their families didn't want them, the schools threw them out, society's been wronged. Nobody in here's got an idea what to do with them and here they are, they come to someone who is not afraid of them, willing to stand up and talk to them and share his home and life with them, and they know him, and they burn him. But I'm not worried about that because I am convinced in my heart that somewhere along the way, this isn't going to happen.

I can explain to you, Your Honor, and did in a letter, what a coach's life is like in the spring. Neither one of us can turn a screwdriver. We looked at that old building. We looked at it to see if we could put our storage up there. It's dilapidated, we couldn't do it and discussed whether we should go up there and fix anything. Neither one of us could do it, and we are struggling to pay for storage rooms when, if that building had been usable, we'd have done it. It's an indefensible building. It's only covered on three sides. There's one whole side of that building, the front had no doors, there's no way to secure that, for him to secure that when he's away from home.

And somehow I thought along the way the system would protect him and it hasn't. Instead they are the victims in this, and not only them, but the victims are my family. I've got a little gang down the street, they come up in front of our house and attacked us several years ago. I knew who they were. The police came and we worked all through that. Today, they wouldn't have even known about Nance and them down there if he hadn't volunteered to go out of town on Monday. And then when they checked and found out about him, they found out what he was doing up there, they didn't have another conversation with him after that, they go straight to Nance and cut them deals. And it's not happening just here, it is happening all over the country. The country we're supposed to believe in, the law system we should support all our lives.

And I sit here with two parents that might not live until Christmas. I've watched in eighteen months a family that's done nothing but given their lives to other people in service, I've watched it destroyed by a system that recalls the rules and policies and procedures, and there's not a lot of concern here, and I'm not talking about you but—

Court: That's not true—

Mr. Paul Phillips: But it seems to me like that a lot of people it's gone right over their heads. I stand here, I couldn't believe it. I thought when we had a verdict, I thought I knew what was going to happen.

Court: Well, Mr. Phillips, I know your weren't at the trial, but I have to tell you there was very strong circumstantial evidence that made it extremely difficult to believe that your brother was not aware of what was going on.

Mr. Paul Phillips: Your Honor, pardon me, but some of these people that teach about these drug labs, and I've done a little research on them since all of this happened, knowing nothing about it beforehand, they give profiles of places where this happens, and this is the farthest place from that profile. There's no dogs, no guns, nobody ever stepped forth. He didn't produce any evidence that anyone stepped forth and found him selling drugs or buying drugs. They tested negative for using it. As a matter of fact, no one ever named him buy the—saw him buy any ether or metallic bars, whatever those were.

And in the closing remarks, this is unbelievable. A man could stand in front of a court in his closing remarks and accuse two people of being cookers in that the court's—it never was even mentioned in the trial. They weren't accused of that, two other people were. If I were them, I'd be looking for some defamation of character, being accused of something later when it didn't happen. Your Honor, I'm sorry, I've spent—

Court: You don't have to apologize.

Mr. Paul Phillips: I've spent ninety days in tears and crying and praying that somehow God would move in this and do something with your heart or the heart of this man. I've been praying for you Mr. Descussio, that God would do something with you. I know you've had some hardships—

Court: Mr. Phillips, Mr. Phillips—

Mr. Paul Phillips: I'm sorry—

Court: Address me about this, don't turn on the lawyers.

Mr. Paul Phillips: All right. I'm sorry I didn't—I just—I've been praying for him and I've prayed for you and Mr. Moore and everybody. I don't know, maybe—Maybe this is—maybe this is God's will and I'm going to have to learn to accept that.

Court: If, in fact, as you believe, your brother and your sister-in-law are not guilty then that's all you can say is that it must be God's will for some reason. I can't guarantee you we have done a right thing with the jury verdict or what will end up being a sentence in this case. I can't guarantee the right thing about anything I do or you do or anyone else does. We do the best we can with the abilities we have. Your brother was given a fair trial. I know you're not happy with the outcome and I know you hoped for a totally different verdict.

Mr. Paul Phillips: I did.

Court: I can understand that. Your brother has a totally clean criminal history and it is difficult to understand why anyone who worked with kids, as the record indicates he has, or his wife, would be involved in this. Nonetheless, there was substantial proof that he was and that she was and the jury believed it. Now I understand what you are talking about, about Mr. Nance and Mr. Tisdale. Unlike some other cases, though, there was no direct promise of a reduction of their sentence and I don't know that any prosecutor in Missouri would even consider asking the judge to reduce their sentences there under these circumstances. But even if—even if there were, all the evidence anybody felt they could present was presented and the jury reached its verdict and it's the only system we have. It is not perfect, but it is the only one we have.

Mr. Paul Phillips: Well, Your Honor, Mr. Tisdale said he was under the impression-

Court: He did, he said he was under the impression he was going to get immunity.

Mr. Paul Phillips: And the last thing I want to say to you and it's the grounds for—it's the grounds for what he did in dealing with these people, it's the grounds for what I did and we've lived with this for twenty-five years. I ask you for mercy. I don't know how much discretion you've got.

Court: Very little.

Mr. Paul Phillips: But I'll tell you this. God says to those who show mercy he'll give them mercy and to those who show no mercy, there'll be no mercy given. Somewhere along the way, truth will prevail. It may not be in this lifetime but it will prevail and those who have lied, they will answer to a high power than me or this Court or this country. I've heard from all over that you're as fair a man as there is around here, that we couldn't have gotten a more fair man and all my brother asked for was a fair trial. I think there were some things that may not be, but I realize this is not the place to discuss that. I just want to ask you for mercy and to take into consideration as much as you possible can the fact that the letters I know some people wrote because they sent me some copies of them—

Court: I got them.

Mr. Paul Phillips: They cover forty-seven years of the man's life and the picture that those letters portrayed are totally contrary to the picture that Mr. Descussio and this Court—

Court: I agree with that—

Mr. Paul Phillips: And Your Honor, when you start thinking about the credibility of those two men who did the testifying and the credibility of those who wrote the letters, and you put those things, you stack them there side by side, you've got such an unweighted situation, this man's life is not about what's come down here. I hope somewhere in this country, somewhere in this city, our reputations—because we're connected together—our reputations are gone. They've taken the best teacher and coach and most concerned person I know about the youth, he's gone, when there's a profession that's got way too few of these people. And they take them away here when he's done nothing, absolutely nothing, neither one of them have, and you surely are looking at something that is just—it's not—in eighteen months I've seen our whole lives go down the tubes. It's unbelievable. I know we've got procedures and formulas and ways of doing things and they all seem to me to stand in the way of bringing about the truth. And I don't know, I just pray that—I just ask, Your Honor, for all the mercy that you can grant in this case and that you'll consider those letters you received. That's the true picture of who he is not measured in one afternoon, or on the stand by two men who are noted liars. It's not the first time Nance has accused somebody of this in other places. A lot of that didn't come out and a lot of the truth. Maybe if there is another round here when we get another chance, maybe it will. I just pray and if I could get down on my knees and crawl around and squirm, If I could change places with him, I would.

Court: I know you would.

Mr. Paul Phillips: Thank you.

Court: Thank you. Does the government wish to be heard with respect to sentencing?

Mr. Descussio: No, Your Honor. We would submit it. We believe the Court has all the facts it needs to pass an appropriate sentence.

Court: Mr. Moore, would you like—does your client wish to make a statement?

Mr. Moore: Yes, Your Honor, I believe my client does wish to make a statement.

Court: Mr. Phillips?

CHAPTER 53

STATEMENTS FROM THE HEART AT SENTENCING (JACK PHILLIPS)

Mr. Jack Phillips: I am just going to say a few things. Like I say, I don't have any experience. There's a lot of things I'd like to say in regards to the case and the testimony.

Court: I wouldn't let you do that.

Mr. Jack Phillips: I'm going to say that—I'm going to say something about my wife. Only this period of time from May of 1996 until July of 1997, she wasn't really there. She was gone more than she was there.

Court: She indicated at one point that she was not there for ten months during 1995.

Mr. Jack Phillips: During 1996, that is correct.

Court: 1995 is what I wrote.

Mr. Jack Phillips: She left me—she left in 1995 in October but I moved into the house in 1996, and one place Mr. Nance mentioned that things started early in 1996 and in the year 1996 she came to the house two and a half weeks in July or early August and then she came back to the house around the first of November.

And with Thanksgiving and Christmas, she spent the last part of November and most of the month of December back in Arkansas, and she didn't officially come back home and stay until April of 1997. She had her own—she had a job in Arkansas, as a matter of fact, a job at a grocery store through July of 1997—I mean 1996. She had a job there and she kept her own mailbox, post office, there, although she didn't have her own residence after 1996 and 1997. She stayed with her sister and my daughter as my sister-in-law testified in Court, and she had her own mailbox through April of 1997 when she came back home. And, Your Honor, if she was accused of purchasing ether, there's no—absolutely no evidence that she ever did, except an accusation. She was accused of washing dishes and I submit we had an electric dishwasher and if she ever washed a dish for those guys, it was because there was something in that dishwasher that she didn't know was there and she just turned it on. Her name wasn't even mentioned ten times in this trial and even in some of the times it was mentioned, it was obvious she wasn't living in Memphis, she was living in Arkansas, she had a job, even had her own home, and I would submit—I would ask that you take that into consideration in regard to her.

I'm sorry the Court had to go through this. I'm thankful that the day of the fire nobody got hurt. I'm thankful that none of the firemen got hurt and I think it came out at trial that my dad was a fireman for many, many, many years and I'm certainly glad no one got hurt. I'm certainly sorry for the pain I've caused my family. Whether I'm guilty or innocent, my family has suffered greatly, and I'm sorry. I've had great support, we've had great support from both our families. They absolutely believe in our innocence.

I want to speak a minute—I've never been in this system or situation. I want to speak with you for a minute about the men that I've been incarcerated with. Your Honor, there's some things going on that somebody's got to address sometime. There's some things that are going on that are unethical and immoral, even for the guilty men. There are some things going on in the legal profession. The things these men are having to do to try to do on their own because their lawyers won't help them, their own lawyers. I know Mr. Hawkins is on his fourth set of lawyers. The lack of effort that's been given to the defense of many of these men, even the ones that readily admit they are guilty, the lack of defense on their behalf is perverting the whole thing of justice. There's people lining up. You can't even talk about your case openly, you have to be very discretionary because people are jumping on people's cases. It happened this week, and everybody knows they really don't know anything about it, they're jumping on to get their sentence reduced.

And even in my case, in our case, if any of the investigators made any effort to interrogate Mr. Boone, who they testified was there the day of the fire and the man's never been questioned. The DEA had an informant working with Mr. Nance and Tisdale during the same time my wife and I are indicted. From May of 1996 until July 1997, they had a DEA informant working with them in Missouri. Over twenty cooks in six of eight counties in Missouri and them acquiring supplies everywhere to do that. Mr. Tisdale and Mr. Nance became so proficient, according to the DEA informant, they could set their labs up in less than three hours, and they would never leave labs set up, it wasn't their nature.

In our situation, all of the empty either cans, the empty fuel things, I don't have a doubt they were put there, but those things weren't scattered around the house before the fire, not the way it was portrayed in the film and videos. Those things came from the upstairs or they had placed the pill packets out by the trash barrel during the course of the weekend when they were cooking. My wife and I, as you know from the trial, were in Alabama that weekend while they maintained we were running errands. She was cooking for them and running errands and I was purchasing pills and supposedly cooking flea powder. That was their testimony and you know that Agent March said that he investigated and we were in Alabama that weekend, and he didn't say he went to Kentucky to see if we were there, like we said we were. He didn't know who we were going to see because he never asked. And obviously, we weren't doing what we were supposed to be doing that weekend of the fire, and if they put the bag of pills—the pill containers out there, I don't know. The ether cans and all that, was spread out around the house and that was all contained in the shed. That was all put out there after the fire. The yard wasn't a wreck like it looked like in the videos where it was obvious there was stuff going on. It wasn't obvious.

And for the amount of time at our age that we are looking at, this is a life sentence for us and we're from a little small town. This is the first time in my life I've gone four months without seeing Kara since I was two years old. Her dad had a business next door to my mom's business and I saw her everyday as a little girl, and it's been tough. And if we had two reliable witnesses giving two consistent testimonies and everybody that's been implicated had been charged, I wouldn't have any problem about this. But we've got at least four statements from Mr. Tisdale—I mean Mr. Nance, at least two from Mr. Tisdale, and their testimonies don't even corroborate each other. You can lay them down side by side of their own testimonies and there's different names, different places, different dates because they weren't involved in our lives.

It came out in Court, us being from the same town that I had coached Mr. Nance, taught school where he went school. I moved—we moved from Rector and came to Memphis in 1975. He was nine years old. I've never taught school in Arkansas, I never coached a game in Arkansas. We left there when he was nine years old and we spent the next twenty years raising our kids, living our life and coaching. My son graduated in 1994. All through the nineties to the day he graduated, he was playing a hundred baseball games a year. We had February to August, playing football from August through November, basketball after that, and we spent all our time at every one of those games. We didn't even have time to go home on weekends. I had no personal relationship with Mr. Nance; I didn't see him again until 1995. Somebody told me who he was; I hadn't seen him since he was nine years old. I saw him one other time in a mall at Christmas in 1995 and saw him in a driveway in 1996. That's the extent of my relationship with Mr. Nance. As far as Arkansas goes, they never came to my house until the spring of 1997. Their testimonies, although may be believed by the jury, just lay them down and look at them, Your Honor, you can see what you've got right there.

Court: I have looked at them and there are some inconsistencies. I know you know enough about the justice system that your brother is worried about now, and I understand why he might be, to know that it is not my function to determine whether your are guilty or not, I haven't done that.

Mr. Jack Phillips: I understand.

Court: And I hope that—I want to say God, I hope they weren't wrong, but if they were, then hopefully somehow or another it will come to the forefront at the appropriate time. If not—I have been overwhelmed by the support that you two have gotten from your family and friends.

Mr. Jack Phillips: We're very grateful for that.

Court: I've tried a lot of cases in the last eleven years, and with the exception of a political case, I have never gotten so much mail on one case and never so much in support of defendants in a criminal trial.

Mr. Jack Phillips: We're grateful for that.

Court: You ought to be. No matter what happens here today, it's an amazing outpouring. On the other hand, the jury found you guilty and, given that my job is to sentence you and I'm—my job is not to second guess the jury.

Mr. Jack Phillips: Yes, sir. I'd like you to take into account, and I know you've already ruled on the amount. Maybe this is not the appropriate time to ask, but there's nothing to indicate, no evidence whatsoever, with the amount of cans, amount of pill boxes or anything, that there's enough of any one ingredient to make three kilos of this drug. There's nobody in this room who knows how much it takes to make three kilos of this drug; of ether, metal, or pills. It's totally subjective. There's just nobody in the room who can testify that there was anything there on that property or in that lab. There's nobody that can testify that a person could make three kilos of this drug or that three kilos of this drug was ever made there. No evidence has been given, no expert called. Nobody's talked about the amounts of ether or the pills, and there's nobody in the room can say there's anything there to make three kilos, or twenty kilos, or thirty grams, there's no evidence presented as to amounts.

I know, Your Honor, in rare cases, in exceptional cases, you won't consider the amount of drugs, that you can downward departure. I know it has to be an exceptional case. Sir, this is an exceptional case. In our forty years of living the best we could, it has got to mean something. We didn't run and I did give you the names of everyone I've known who has been involved with this drug, and that eventually it all led to Sam Nance. And Mr. Tisdale testified he had signed a proffer agreement and he did testify he thought he was under immunity, but the point being, these guys had something to gain. I tried to—I don't know what I could have done under the circumstances once the fire started. I don't now what I could have done differently that would have led to a different outcome. And if I did anything wrong before that fire, it wasn't because I was intentionally trying to break the law or be involved with anything illegal just because I made poor judgments about some people or was blinded to their faults, it was because I was trying to do the right thing. Thank you.

Court: Thank you, sir.

Mr. Moore: Your Honor, in light of the relationship may I defer to Mrs. Phillips and reserve comments after this?

Court: Yes sir.

CHAPTER 54

STATEMENTS FROM THE HEART AT SENTENCING (KARA PHILLIPS AND JUNE RILEY)

Court: Ms. Phillips, do you—Ms. Riley, does Ms. Phillips wish to say anything?

Ms. Riley: Just a minute, please.

(brief pause)

Ms. Riley: As the Court might have noticed, Ms. Phillips is in a highly emotional state and she had written out a statement before she came here with the Court's permission, I will read it on her behalf.

Court: That will be fine.

Ms. Riley: Thank you, Your Honor.

"My name is Kara Phillips. I'm writing this letter to inform you of my status. I am forty-five years old. I've been incarcerated since August of 1998. I don't do nor have I done drugs or alcohol. I have a wonderful family, who throughout this crisis has shown unconditional love and support. My mom, who is ill, has made arrangements to remodel her home for me to reside with her. My sister, who was diagnosed with MD, muscular dystrophy, has agreed as well. I have four grandchildren and other family members in Arkansas and Missouri. We are a close family. I have never had any run-ins with the law. These four months of incarceration have given me a lot of time to myself. I have had time to think a lot. I don't have any hatred nor am I angry at anyone who has put me here. I realize everybody has a job to do. Being incarcerated has taught me a lot. I've learned to cherish my freedom, value my family and that God is my all-in-all. If I have to do more time or even if I get probation or even house arrest, I can do it because I've learned through every experience I go through, I can either die from it or grow from it. So I ask that Your Honor have mercy on sentencing me. Whatever I'm sentenced to, this experience has changed my life."

Court: Do you want to add anything?

Ms. Riley: Your Honor, I might be out of order, I don't know if Mr. Moore—first, Your Honor, I'd like to make a remark about Mr. Paul Phillips. Since before the trial, during the trial, and after the trial, Mr. Phillips has been very active in the defense of both Phillips. He's assisted in any way that he could, along with members of the family, but Mr. Phillips has been especially active. Following the conviction, Mr. Paul Phillips embarked on an avid investigation himself, wrote a number of memorandum to me and to Mr. Moore. I believe he sent identical copies each time to both of us asking us to follow up on various leads that he secured after talking to various people. He did his best to follow up on possible things that should have happened at trial, or that might happen post trial. I would have to subdivide results of his efforts into possible things that should have happened at trial, which later may be grounds of a post conviction petition, things that might be useful for an appeal or for a motion for a new trial, and some things which may be useful at sentencing. There's nothing that's not useful in some respect or in some category that I think we've presented the Court with as much as we could in this—at this hearing—that Mr. Paul Phillips was able to find. We haven't had an opportunity to discuss with him how some stuff cannot be retried or is not usable in the sense that it is not admissible, but I want to apologize to him if he thinks that, at any time, I did not think his contribution was very valuable. There were just times when I couldn't have a full conversation with him on the phone or when I couldn't respond to him point by point in his correspondence.

But he—I know the Court has remarked in the volume of material the Court has received from various family members and friends. I was overwhelmed, too, by family members and friends, and especially by Mr. Phillip's activities in trying to help his brother and his brother's wife. I want to offer my appreciation to him for that.

As far as law—excuse me, Your Honor, I find that very often my defendants arouse my nurturing instincts and she's done that with me. In spite of the fact that she is an adult and a grandmother, I feel like she's very naïve in the ways of the world in some respects, especially with what this milieu is, and that's not grounds for the Court to depart downward, but I'd respectfully ask the Court to consider a minimal sentence for Mrs. Phillips. Whatever happens, I don't think the Court's going to ever hear from Mrs. Phillips again. Thank you.

CHAPTER 55

STATEMENTS FROM THE HEART AT SENTENCING (LESTER MOORE)

Court: Mr. Moore?

Mr. Moore: Your Honor, as a lawyer, this is probably one of the hardest things we have to do is address the Court at the sentencing of a client. I think, though, I haven't had to sit there, it's got to be hard for a judge, too, because from time to time we come upon people who find themselves convicted in the sight of the law under whatever circumstances and they become part of the system and probably worse than that is—and I won't get into a criticism of the sentencing guidelines—but obviously I recognize the Court's got little discretion. It's not a situation where you always take into account, as Mr. Paul Phillips said, forty-seven years of someone's life. Even if we presume that the jury said at least two of those years were not exemplary, the Court's note from letters and I think the record speaks for itself that Mr. Jack Phillips has done a lot of good work with the other forty-five years. I ask you to take that into account. I recognize, as I say, the restraints. It's very hard for Mr. Phillips and for the family, for people who aren't involved in this system to understand the restraints that are put on both the Court, and family as Ms. Riley and I at this state of the procedures. But we ask the court to consider and give frankly Mr. and Mrs. Phillips every benefit of the doubt you can, every consideration that you can, and to sentence them at the very minimum sentence that the law allows under the circumstances.

We ask the Court to, as I say, to look at the contributions heretofore, made by them. I am not going to rehash the evidence, I'm not going to rehash the trial because this isn't the time or place, but I would submit to the Court that if you could see how these people lived, if you could see what assets they have, and that if we are to believe the testimony of the government's witnesses, you can't help but wonder what happened to the proceeds, to the money that should have been made from all those drugs. There's no proof in the record that Mr. and Mrs. Phillips were on drugs, were drug addicted. There's certainly no evidence they were living high, enjoying the benefits of being drug dealers. There's no evidence they gave the money to—or had it stashed for close family members, residents, or had it invested in a false name. I just submit to the Court it's a very tragic situation and I ask you to consider, as I say, sentencing at the very minimum you can.

CHAPTER 56

JUDGE JASON T. BURNS SPEAKS

Court: Thank you counsel, Mr. and Mrs. Phillips both. Mr. Moore referred to the fact that we are governed in a large part by what we call the United States Sentencing Guidelines Manual, and that is true. That is a manual of sentencing maximums and minimums, a range from which the judge is allowed to choose a sentence for reasons to be stated in the record. We do, in fact, under extraordinary circumstances have authority to depart from those ranges, but these extraordinary circumstances are not because we disagree with the jury verdict or because it is difficult to understand how these defendants could have been involved with drug dealing when, as Mr. Moore says, there is no explanation for the profit and there's an awful lot of evidence that they were involved with the manufacture and sale of drugs. The guidelines simply do not give the Court the authority to depart for those reasons.

It is evident that Mr. and Mrs. Phillips have apparently affected a lot of people's lives in a positive manner. Nothing else, I think, accounts for the outpouring of support I have received which will be made part of the record. And there are discrepancies, in fact, that are difficult to understand when you try to evaluate whether the jury reached the right verdict in this case or not. Certainly not the least of which— not the least of which is the fact that the primary evidence, strongest evidence, in the case was the testimony of Mr. Nance and Mr. Tisdale. But there was also strong circumstantial evidence of another nature that was not tied to their testimony at all.

Our system is not perfect. Nothing that man has ever done or created or planned is perfect. I would love to think that nothing goes through this Court that is ever going to come out wrong. I'm not that naïve. There are times when the juries and this Court will make mistakes and there are times when I will make mistakes but even that is no basis for me to say I will disregard the guidelines in this case. And were I to do so, I would simply be doing exactly what the defendants are accused of doing, and that is ignoring the law. As I said earlier, and I know most of you understand our system of justice, a group of citizens are called as jurors and they hear the evidence and it is their job to determine whether the case has been proven or not. The jury did that in this case, and they did it unanimously. My authority does not permit me to disregard that jury verdict under the circumstances that are in front of me today. As I said a little while ago to Mr. Phillips, I almost want to say I hope the jury was wrong because I don't want to see the system fail. On the other hand, I will say that there's a lot of questions in my mind about this particular case.

Now Mrs. Phillips, you suggested a downward departure. I think I tried to explain to you that I do not have the facts in front of me which permit me to depart downward. I do have the authority within the range, which we will discuss in a moment.

CHAPTER 57

THE ACTUAL SENTENCE

Court: The guidelines in this case place…call for an offense level of 39 with respect to Mr. Phillips. He has no criminal history of any kind and therefore in the lowest criminal history category I. Primarily—well, not primarily—because of the offense level involved in this case, the sentencing guidelines call for a sentence of between 262 months and 327 months of imprisonment. There is a minimum sentence under the statute of 120 months on Count 1, a maximum on Count 2 of 120, and a maximum on Count 3 of 240 months imprisonment. Count 1 requires a supervised release period after incarceration of five years. Count 2 and 3 call for two-or two to three years. There is a fine range of twenty-five thousand to four million dollars and a three hundred dollar special assessment.

In Kara Phillips's case, she is an offense level of 34 because it has been determined that she was a minor participant. She had no criminal history either and is at the low criminal history category of I. Those two factors call for a sentence of 168 months to 210 months imprisonment. Count 1 requires a minimum of 120, Count 2 has a maximum of 120. Count 1 calls for a supervised release of five years and count

2 two to three years. The fine range in her case is twenty million—excuse me—twenty thousand to four million dollars. Any legal objections to the findings of the Court by the government?

Mr. Descussio: No, Your Honor.

Court: Mr. Moore?

Mr. Moore: No, Your Honor.

Court: Ms. Riley?

Ms. Riley: Your Honor, I can't remember if I—I may not have addressed the issue of a fine—I submit to the Court that Mrs. Phillips—

Court: There is no evidence in this case that would support the defendants have the ability to pay a fine.

Ms. Riley: Thank you, Your Honor.

Court: I know that those of you in the courtroom that are here for the Phillips are convinced that they were not involved and I do not question your ability to judge this matter in your own mind. I will say that in different circumstances, I might well go to the maximum sentence in this case because drugs, as you now Mr. Phillips, probably have done more damage to this country than perhaps anything other than our lose of values. On the other hand, I will not disregard the fact that neither defendant has a criminal history of any kind, despite having lived into their mid forties and both have testaments from a number of people that they have done a good work for people that otherwise might not have gotten help. Because of that, the Court intends to sentence the defendants to the minimum sentences of incarceration. I nonetheless, recognize that this is a horrendous sentence.

In Mr. Phillips's case, it is the intent of the Court to impose the minimal guideline sentence of 262 months. On Count 1, 120 months, concurrent. On Count 2, 240 months, concurrent. On Count 3, concurrent. A five year period of supervised release on Count 1 and a three year period on Count 2 and 3. No fine will be imposed, a three hundred dollar assessment is required.

In Mrs. Phillips's case, again, I choose to sentence at the low end of the guidelines for the reasons stated. 168 months of incarceration on Count 1, 120 months on Count 2, concurrent on Count 2. Supervised release is the same as I instructed with regard to Mr. Phillips and the Court will impose no fine. There is a two hundred dollar assessment. Are there any legal objections to the intended sentence, reserving to the defendants, of course, all objections that have been made today and overruled.

Mr. Moore: Nothing further, Your Honor. I did want to take up with the Court about, obviously, I think the financial matter set out that Mr. and Mrs. Phillips are literally bankrupt. They have no assets at this time and I would ask the Court to declare Mr. Phillips indigent.

Court: Well, you will need to file an appropriate petition and we will address it at that time. Formally, then, pursuant to the Sentencing Reform Act of 1994, it is the judgment of the Court that the defendant Jack Phillips is herby sentenced to a period of imprisonment of 262 months in the custody of the Bureau of Prisons. Upon his release from imprisonment, the defendant will be placed on supervised release for a term—excuse me, I should restate that 262 months on Count 1, 120 months on Count 2, 240 months concurrent on Count 3. Upon his release from imprisonment, the defendant will be placed on supervised release for a term of five years on Count 1 and three years concurrent on Counts 2 and 3. Within seventy-two hours of his release from the custody of the Bureau of Prisons, the defendant shall report to the probation office in the district in which he is released. A three hundred dollar assessment is adjudged against the defendant payable to the United States of America immediately.

And pursuant to the Sentencing Reform Act of 1994, it is the judgment of the Court that the defendant, Kara Phillips, is herby committed to the custody of the Bureau of Prisons to be imprisoned for a term of 168 months on Count 1 and 120 months concurrent on Count 2. Upon release from imprisonment, Mrs. Phillips shall report to the probation office in the district to which she is released. A two hundred dollar assessment is adjudged against the defendant payable to the United States of America immediately.

Mr. Phillips and Mrs. Phillips, you do have the right to appeal the verdict that was rendered in this case by the jury. You have the right to appeal this sentence if it has been illegally imposed, if it has been imposed as a result of miscalculation of the guideline range, and if it is plainly unreasonable. In order to appeal, you must file a notice of appeal with ten days after the written judgment in this case. Both of your lawyers will advise you in that respect and if you elect to appeal, they will file a motion of appeal for you. You are both entitled to retain counsel of your own choosing if you are able. If you are unable and file the appropriate petition, counsel will be appointed for you at no cost to you. If you are indigent, and that is shown to the Court, you will be allowed to appeal without payment of any cost. In Mr. Phillips's case, Mr. Moore, if in fact a petition is filed or is needed to be filed, of course we expect you to file it.

Mr. Moore: Yes, Your Honor, I'll do that.

Court: We've had no discussion, of course, up until this time about whether there is any particular place that the defendants would prefer to serve this sentence. I do not have the authority to dictate that, I do have the power to recommend to the Bureau of Prisons.

Sometimes they listen, sometimes they don't for various reasons. Ms. Riley?

Ms. Riley: Mrs. Phillips would like to be closer to her family in Arkansas, Your Honor, if that is possible.

Mr. Moore: Your Honor, on behalf of Mr. Phillips, if he could stay close to here, he'd prefer to do that.

Court: Stay close to what?

Mr. Moore: Stay close to here, Memphis. You know the relationship with his brother who lives here, that would be his preference.

Court: Ms. Hurt, let me see you up here a moment.
(discussion between the judge and probation officer, Ms. Hurt)

Court: There is a female prison facility in Lexington, Kentucky. So far as I know this is the closest one for Mrs. Phillips.

Ms. Riley: Yes, Your Honor.

Court: Okay, I'll make that recommendation and in the event there is not one closer, I'll recommend Lexington. That is also a minimum facility. I do not know if she will qualify for that because of the amount of drugs in this conviction. It is also a medical facility and I think that would be of some assistance. In Mr. Phillips's case, I'm willing to recommend he be sentenced to a facility close to Memphis. Mr. Descussio, do you know of a reason why the Court should not recommend Millington?

Mr. Descussio: I'm not sure that he's going to be eligible—I don't—I mean, I have no objection to the Court recommending Millington.

Court: All right. I'm going to recommend Millington. Again, however, I do not know if he will qualify for Millington and that is a decision the Bureau of Prison has to make. Do either of the defendants have any questions about the appeal rights that were just mentioned to them procedurally?

Ms. Riley: I intend to file a motion of appeal for Mrs. Phillips, Your Honor. We may still think about filing a motion for a new trial prior to that so it will be within a short period.

Mr. Moore: No, Your Honor, there's no question from us.

Court: I will file these letters that have been sent to the Court on behalf of the defendants. They will be part of the file for any purposes necessary. With respect to those of you that are here, I will tell you I know that this is a grievous moment for you, but, nonetheless, I appreciate the fact that you are here. You would not believe how many times we have sentencings of this caliber when on one shows up. I would say eighty percent of the time, if not more. Your support is important to both these people and although you are terribly disappointed with the verdict in this case, your continued support, no doubt, will be of assistance. If there's nothing else, the Court is adjourned.

GOOD-BYE, KARA

When the judge announced our sentences, Kara looked at me and smiled. She almost looked relieved. She said, "One hundred sixty-eight months. That's not much, is it?" I was so stunned I couldn't speak.

I had just been sentenced to 262 months. I did the quick math in my head: over twenty-one years. For Kara, fourteen years. I just looked at Kara.

As the smile faded, she said, "Jack, how long is 168 months?"

I told her, "Fourteen years."

She looked like I had hit her in the face. She almost fell right out of her seat in front of my eyes. As tears streamed down her face, she said, "How many years did you get, Jack?"

I said, "Almost twenty-two years, Kara."

She broke down and wept and cried, "Oh my God, Jack! Oh my God!"

I hugged her and whispered, "I'm so sorry, Kara!"

The weeping between us was minor compared to what was going on in the gallery among those there to support us. Between Mary Lynn, our family, and our friends, there was a total outpouring of emotion that filled the entire space of the large courtroom.

I was shaken to my core. To see my wife, Kara, go to prison for fourteen years for something she didn't even do! My God! How was

I supposed to process that? How had this happened to us? How had things gone so wrong?

No one in the courtroom was more devastated than Paul. His little brother was in trouble, and he couldn't protect him. Mom had told him to watch over me when I was born. He always had. He had always tried to make things right for me. He was completely overwhelmed. And hurt. He hurt for me. He hurt for Kara. He hurt for the gap that was going to be left in his life.

After court was adjourned, our closest family members came up and hugged us quickly. Paul said, "Don't worry, we'll get you out." I told him, "Paul, it won't be that easy." Our friends waved and encouraged us to stay strong. We were so stunned that we couldn't say or do much.

Our attorneys told us they would file the notices of appeal and be in contact. Lester said he would be right up so we could spend some time together as he promised.

The US marshals handcuffed us and led us out of the courtroom. We were taken to the elevator and then to another floor. I don't know if we went up or down. It didn't matter much now. What did matter was Kara. We ignored the marshals and talked and kissed and told each other how much we loved the other one, and we both tried to encourage each other.

When we got off the elevator, we turned down a short hall. There were offices with doors of half glass on each side of the hallway. We were taken into the office on the right side of the hallway. It had a long counter (as did the office on the other side of the hallway) like a person might find at a DMV office. The marshals told us to say good-bye. I told them that our attorney was coming, but they just looked at me.

We told each other good-bye. I kissed Kara and looked her in the eyes and said, "Stay strong, Kara, and live through this. We'll do what we can to get out."

Kara nodded her head yes as tears streamed down her face, and she said, "I love you, Jack," just like she had said to me a million times before. It had never meant so much!

I told her, "I love you too, Kara."

One of the marshals took her by the right elbow, walked to the door, crossed the hallway, and went through the door on the other side. They continued walking the length of the counter in that office. I kept watching and hoping Kara would turn around so I could see her face one more time. She never turned around. I watched her walk away from me until she reached the end of the counter, and then they turned left and were gone. It was December 5, 1998. I wondered if I would ever see Kara again. I felt like the death angel had passed between us.

The author would classify himself as a teacher and a coach. He has a BS in education (with a double major in history/social studies) and an MA in secondary education administration and supervision. He has spent much of his life in front of a classroom or a team on a field, court, or track. He coached football with his older brother for almost twenty years, fulfilling a lifetime dream. He has been married to his high school sweetheart for forty-five years. The author would describe himself as just a normal man with a normal family. He and his wife have two children, five grandchildren, and one great-grandchild. The author and his wife are Christians who had gone through a severe trial that would test their faith and disrupt their life of normalcy. It also tested the fabric of their character.

CPSIA information can be obtained
at www.ICGtesting.com
Printed in the USA
LVOW11s0240150218
566705LV00001B/7/P